The Mystery Fancier

Volume 7, Number 6
November/December 1983

TABLE OF CONTENTS

MYSTERIOUSLY SPEAKING	Page 1
A Few Kind Words for Ashton-Kirk By Bob Sampson	Page 3
The Violent World of Mike Hammer By Jim Traylor	Page 13
The Old Man in the Corner By Earl F. Bargainnier	Page 21
C.B. Greenfield: The Metaphor Is the Man By Jane S. Bakerman	Page 24
VERDICTS Book Reviews	Page 30
THE DOCUMENTS IN THE CASE Letters	Page 43

The Mystery Fancier
(USPS:428-590)
is edited and published bi-monthly by
Guy M. Townsend
1711 Clifty Drive
Madison, IN 47250

SUBSCRIPTION RATES: Second-class mail, U.S. and Canada, $12.00 per year (6 issues); first-class mail, U.S. and Canada, $15.00; overseas surface mail, $12.00; overseas air mail, $18.00. Overseas subscribers please pay in international money order, check drawn on U.S. bank, or currency; no checks drawn on foreign banks, please.

Single copy price: $2.50
Second-class postage paid at Madison, Indiana
Copyright 1982 by Guy M. Townsend
All rights reserved for contributors
ISSN:0146-3160

Covers by Brad W. Foster

Some people are just never satisfied. You'd think that a fellow with enough letters behind his name to make a respectable bowl of alphabet soup would be crazy to go back to school to get another degree, and you'd be right, especially when that fellow is a decrepit forty years of age. But I didn't get to be rich and famous by letting public opinion stand in my way, so this past August I enrolled as a part-time student in the Salmon P. Chase School of Law, located in northern Kentucky, just across the river from Cincinnati. Chase isn't exactly Harvard Law, but it is close enough (just barely) for me to commute back and forth and still hold down a full-time job here in Madison. But, Lord, does it take time! The round-trip commute (three times a week) is just over 150 miles, and, what with driving, attending classes, and studying, I find myself with virtually no free time on my hands for such things as editing and publishing TMF. Since I am committed to the idiocy of finishing law school (provided, of course, that I don't flunk out), I thought at first of simply putting TMF in cold storage for the three or four (probably four) years that I'll be otherwise engaged. I hated the thought of letting it die altogether, and a temporary suspension of publication, effective with this issue, seemed to be the best course of action I could take. Then I remembered an offer made by that noted Chicagoland raconteur and voyeur, John Nieminski, when I threatened to shut down operations several years ago. John had offered to take it over if I decided to give it up, so I called him up and asked if he, like Barkis, was willing. Since John just happens to be about the best non-professional writer/editor on earth, I knew that I was taking an awful chance, but as it happened he had other commitments and had to pass up the opportunity of showing me up for the pedestrian hacker that I really am.

With John out of the picture, I began laying in a store of mothballs preparatory to folding and storing the TMF tent when I chanced to mention my decision to that bearded Boy Wonder, Steve Stilwell, the state of whose mental condition I leave you to deduce from the fact that he loves Minneapolis and hates winter. Steve, who has made a second career out of pointing out my mistakes to me with a gentleness and sensitivity worthy of Torquemada himself, refused to listen to reason and ultimately offered to take over the lion's share of the work, at least for the duration of my four-year sentence to law school, if I would keep TMF alive. As I was already having bad feelings about being completely divorced from TMF, I gave in without much of a struggle.

So, as of the next issue (8:1), Steve will take over the editorial duties, and I will continue to handle all the other duties--publishing, mailing, and subscriptions. All articles, reviews, and letters to the editor should henceforth be mailed to Steve at 3004 E. 25th St., Minneapolis, MN 55406. All subscription queries, complaints about issues not received, and checks--especially all checks--should be mailed to me at the old 1711 Clifty Drive address.

Some of you may be leery about continuing your subscriptions, or submitting contributions, under an as yet unknown editorship--although, God knows, if you've put up with my editorial capriciousness over the past seven years the unknown should hold no terrors for you--but I assure you that I would shut down the magazine altogether before I would turn it over to someone in whom I did not have full confidence. As most of you know, Steve is the compiler of the ten-year index to TAD; a smaller number of you also know him as one of the better contributors to DAPA-EM. He is extremely knowledgeable about mysteries in general and delights in pointing out holes in my knowledge of Nero Wolfe lore. He is brash, opinionated, obstinate, ornery, and obnoxious--in other words, you probably won't notice any difference when I'm gone.

Not, of course, that I will be gone altogether. As I get the hang of being a student again, I hope to contribute an occasional review here and carping letter of criticism there. I'll remain on the masthead as publisher and eminence grise, and as time permits I'll give Steve a hand with the editorial duties, if he needs and wants it.

Just how we are going to handle the technical aspects of editing in Minnesota and publishing in Indiana may interest you. As soon as I get these two issues (7:5 and 7:6) together, I am going to pack up this trusty computer and ship it to Minneapolis. (I've already sent Steve several manuals, which probably have him pulling out his hair by now--who writes those things, anyway?) Then I'm going to buy another Kaypro (a 10 this time) for use at this end. Steve will edit the magazine on his computer and send the disks to me. I will print out the hard copy here, paste up the issue, and print it on my trusty Multilith 1250 during my spare time (chuckle).

Which brings us to the question of money. I'm going to be out close to three thousand dollars on the Kaypro 10, so I'd appreciate it if you folks would send in your renewal checks as soon as possible. And while you're at it, how about buying a copy of Nevins and Stanich's **Sound of Detection**? According to John Ball in the January 1984 issue of **MSMM**, "This is a specialist's item, but a very good one for Queen collectors and those interested in what is now known as old time radio." In the January 1984 **EQMM**, Ed Hoch called it "a book that belongs on the shelf of every Queen fan or radio buff." If you need any further convincing, see Marv Lachman's review in TMF (7:5). And, while I'm hawking my wares, may I remind you that the hardbound facsimile edition of the first volume of TAD is still in print? You'll find a place for ordering it on the renewal form. In short, send money--the more of it the better. (Hot damn, I can hardly wait to write my first l.o.c.)

A Few Kind Words for Ashton-Kirk

Bob Sampson

The Lovely Girl: "He's very handsome and very wealthy. comes of a very old family; has the entree into the most exclusive houses, but practically ignores society."

An Eminent Attorney: "A very unusual young man. I might call him acutely intellectual, and he is an adept in many out of the way branches of knowledge. He would make a wonderful lawyer, but has too much imagination. Thinks more of visionary probabilities than of tangible facts."

A Close Friend: "As an amateur actor, Kirk is without an equal. If he adopted the stage, he'd make a sensation. At college he was a most tremendous athlete too--football, cross-country running, wrestling, boxing. And I'm told that he still keeps in training. Clever chap."

The Professor: "I never saw a more splendid natural equipment for languages. The most sprawling dialect seemed a simple matter to him; Greek and the oriental languages were no more trouble in his case than the 'first reader' is to an intelligent child."

A Distant Relation: "I can't fancy his marrying at all. His ways and moods and really preposterous habits would drive a wife mad.... He spends days and nights in positively uncanny chemical experiments. Without a word to anyone he plunges off on some mysterious errand, to be gone for weeks. They do tell me that he is to all intents and purposes a policeman.... He loves to do things that others have tried and failed. Even as a boy he was that way. It was quite discouraging to have a child straighten out little happenings that we had all given up in despair."[1]

The object of this admiring consensus is Mr. Ashton-Kirk, an extraordinary young man who starred, if sparely, in a brief series of mystery novels published from 1910 to 1918. Mr. Ashton-Kirk appears to have no first name, although warm friends call him "Kirk." But in

most other things, he nears perfection, the high noon of Western man.
   He is a very bright young man, indeed. Singular dark eyes gleam from a keen, dark face. "It was an altogether modern countenance...' but for all that, there was something almost mystic in it. It may have been that the mind which weighed and valued so many things, unnoticed by the crowd, had given something of the same touch to the face as the pondering of the secrets of life is said to give to the oriental anchorites."[2]
   But we need not be detained by this amiable hocum. Ashton-Kirk is a perfectly nice young man, whose charm survives the enthusiasm of his author. He is of impeccable lineage. He traces his family back through the centuries. From their interminable excellences, he has inherited that distinction of mind and physique so necessary to qualify as a popular series hero in those remote times.
   He is immensely wealthy. And he is never less than perfectly dressed in unostentatious clothing, carefully pressed. (Unless adventure has sung its giddy song and coaxed him off in some rough disguise.) How then could you guess his secret? Even those singular eyes, whatever that may mean, fail to suggest that, in 1910, he was the newest, most modern, most genetically pure of all the Sherlock Holmes imitators.
   Ashton-Kirk does Holmes with a flair:

> "Crimes are growing no fewer; and if we must have crime I should personally prefer those perpetrators to have some little artistry."

Or you may favor this pleasing exchange:

> **Friend:** "Have you done anything in your line for the Treasury Department lately?"
> **Ashton-Kirk:** "Oh, a small matter of some duplicate plates. It had some interest, but there was nothing extraordinary about it."

Or perhaps you may find this dialogue appealing:

> **Young Lady:** "I am very sorry that I deceived you yesterday morning."
> **Ashton-Kirk:** "I was not deceived; so there was no harm done."

Holmes borrowings, like red sparks, float through these stories.
   Ashton-Kirk, for instance, has a commonplace book--a set of canvas-covered reference books filled with "carefully spaced entries in a copper-plate hand." These are kept up for him by his staff and are supposed to include only uncommon and out-of-the-way information. (When they do not, he is singularly annoyed.)
   When he is not studying his references, or playing in his chemical laboratory, or smoking his Coblentz pipe, or aiding the poor, sluggish authorities, he is toying around in disguise. Ashton-Kirk, that proper young man, loves disguise. At least once a novel, he gets himself up as a street tough, or a sick man, or an Italian laborer with a comic-strip accent. His characterizations are deft as those of Nick Carter, or Holmes himself, for that matter. And, like Holmes, he relishes the instant when the disguise is stripped away, confounding friend and reader alike, although, God knows, they should be prepared for such unexpected wonders.
   Ashton-Kirk's investigations are also in the classical mode. He

flings himself on the carpet. He bends close to the ground. Out with the strong lense, out with bits of paper in which he tenderly encloses little dust samples, his eyes flickering singularly. All the while, he is deducting. From a partly drawn blind, a candle stump, a discharged revolver, a red fragment from a punched railroad ticket. After which, the dazzle:

>**Ashton-Kirk:** "What would you say if I told you that I draw from these (clues) that the gentleman (involved in the crime) was short, well-dressed, near-sighted, and knew something of the modern German dramatists?"

During these excursions into ratiocination, he is usually accompanied by a friend, all agog in the style of Dr. Watson:

>**Friend:** "Now I suppose I'm all kinds of an idiot for not understanding how you know all these things about a man you never saw. But I confess candidly; I **don't** understand."
>**Ashton-Kirk:** "It all belongs to my method of work. It's simple enough when you go about it in the right way."

While Holmes is the great influence, Ashton-Kirk's literary origins contain generous samplings of such other greats as Dupin, Martin Hewitt, Norry the Diplomatic Agent, and Nick Carter. Thus wonderfully compounded, he detected splendidly through four novels: **Ashton-Kirk Investigator** (1910), **Ashton-Kirk Secret Agent** (1912), **Ashton-Kirk Special Detective** (1914), and **Ashton-Kirk Criminologist** (1918).[3] Whether these received prior magazine publication is not known.

The books were written by John Thomas McIntyre. Born in Philadelphia on November 26, 1871, McIntyre was a predestined writer. He first contributed to the Sunday editions of the Philadelphia **Times** and **Press**. He soon developed a flair for stage writing and in 1892 saw produced the first of more than thirty comedies and dramas.

His stage writing, which continued until about 1910, was paralleled by a stream of books. In 1902 he published the novel, **The Ragged Edge** (a tale of ward life and politics and appropriately seamy). This was followed by numerous boys' books, among them **Fighting King George** (1905), **Boy Tars of 1812** (1907), a multi-volume series titled **With [famous name] at [famous place]** and **The Young Continentals at [various sites from Bunker Hill to Lexington]** (four books from 1909 to 1912).

In 1908 McIntyre entered the mystery field with **In the Dead of Night**. After the Ashton-Kirk series, he wrote the gangster novel **Slag** (1927) and the mystery, **The Museum Murder** (1929). He also published articles in various magazines of the 'Teens, including **McBrides'**, **Scribners'**, and **Colliers'**. His main effort, however, was toward the historical novel. In this field his books included **Blowing Weather** (1923), **Shot Towers** (1926), **Stained Sails** (1928), and **Drums in the Dawn** (1932). In 1936 he was the United States winner in the All-Nations Prize Novel Competition, the book being **Steps Going Down** (1938), the prize being $4,000. Many of these works contained roughly realistic material, biting enough to jar his contemporaries, who had not got used to Upton Sinclair or Stephen Crane, either.

In 1939 McIntyre created the series detective Jerry Mooney, who first appeared in **Mooney Moves Around** (1939); other series titles include **Death Strikes at Heron House, Death at Daker,** and **Ninth Floor: Middle City Tower**. All Mooney mysteries were signed with the pseudonym Kerry O'Neil.

After 1943 McIntyre does not seem to have published further books. He died on May 21, 1951, in Philadelphia at the age of seventy-nine.

The Ashton-Kirk volumes, then, are barely a flicker in an extended career. They begin as the immense surge of McIntyre's stage writing ebbs and after a burst of boys' books. It is as if he were testing himself against increasingly complex forms of composition--although the truth is likely more prosaic, involving nothing more wonderful than the opening of new fiction markets. In retrospect, the sequence of events in any life seems purposeful, when in reality accident, undescribed and unremembered, shaped it all.

Ashton-Kirk Investigator (1910) is concerned with the murder of the leering, twisted, sadistic Hume, the numismatist--who also collected pictures of Mad Anthony Wayne. Hume is found in his antique-crammed rooms; he has been stabbed through with a bayonet. From this encouraging situation, the problem grows wildly tangled as McIntyre trots out a string of terribly suspicious characters--the silent girl, the young man all knotted in guilty secrets, the hot-tempered street musician, the mysterious deaf-mute.

As usual, the feminine lead has a secret. in her dim way, she is determined not to tell. For her true love may be endangered if.... And so it goes. Each Ashton-Kirk novel contains one of these lovely bubbleheads. It is her responsibility to stretch the soup to 330 pages. And so she thrusts herself into suspicious circumstances, clogs the action with ill-timed secrets, becomes coldly aloof when questioned. Not for anything would she do anything sensible.

But all the characters have something to hide. Nothing much, but something. All dart about, their mouths stained by deceit, no flicker of common sense lighting their behavior. Had any one of them shown the least gleam of intelligence, the story would have ended on page 50.

As it is, the story yaps passionately after each character in turn. So do the police: if this one is not guilty, that one must be. All the while the clues shower down. Each clue is discovered, exclaimed over to the staccato of Ashton-Kirk's deductions. He sprays these out like a man watering a garden.

--What was hidden behind the picture?
--What had the violinist hidden beneath his coat?
--Why was a shot heard, although the victim was stabbed?
--What message was concealed in the candle drippings?
--What was the code of the gloves?
--Why are the police so infernally thick?

It all seems faintly silly when described. However, in spite of all, the story lopes wonderfully along, propelled by deductions and Ashton-Kirk's little sermons and all that premeditated confusion. If the story never really goes anywhere, it travels in stylish circles. At first it really seems that you are reading something with content. Only later does it all vaporize, leaving behind only a faint memory. but you never lose faith in Ashton-Kirk:

> **Friend (to Ashton-Kirk):** "You go prancing about so like a conjurer that there's not a moment that I don't expect something. If you finish by dragging the murderer from your sleeve, I'll not be at all astonished."

The motive for all this furor involves stolen plans for a

heavier-than-air machine and the punishment of a wretch who betrayed a diamond-smuggling gang. (Revelation of these facts in no way compromises the ending of the story for contemporary readers, assuming that there are any; these motives are casually flipped out to justify all the previous commotion.)

Of **Ashton-Kirk Investigator, A Catalogue of Crime** remarks:

> This author acquired a certain reputation as a practitioner of the realistic novel before the first world war. As a writer of detective fiction, he is not precisely a realist, but rather an imitator of Doyle and Arthur Morrison, whom he resembles in his dual literary role but scarcely approaches in quality.[4]

True enough that when compared to the richness of Sherlock Holmes, Ashton-Kirk seems rather transparent and precious. His adventures are carefully wound up, like plastic walking toys, and set to hobbling about to the whirring of the spring. This mechanical energy is almost as annoying as Ashton-Kirk's glossy excellence. For all that, he is a rather pleasing character, modest for a change, and essentially nice. He is the most amiable of detectives. He makes Albert Campion look like a sourpuss.

Every series detective benefits from a distinctive home base. Ashton-Kirk has one. He lives in a distinguished row house, faced with alternating black and white brick, set squarely in a boiling slum:

> Old-fashioned streets alter wonderfully after the generations of elect have passed; but when Eastern Europe takes to dumping its furtive hordes into one, the change is marked indeed. In this one peddler's wagons replaced the shining carriages of a former day--wagons drawn by large-jointed horses and driven by bearded men who cried their wares in strange, throaty voices.
>
> Everything exhaled a thick, semi-oriental smell. Dully painted fire-escapes clung hideously to the fronts of buildings; stagnant-looking men, wearing their hats, leaned from bedroom windows. the once decent hallways were smutted with grimy hands; the wide marble steps were huddled with alien, unclean people.
>
> A splendidly spired church stood almost shoulder to shoulder with the Ashton-Kirk house.... Years of neglect had made it unwholsome and cavern-like; and finally it was given over to a tribe of stolid Lithuanians who stuck a cheaply gilded Greek cross over the door and thronged the street with their wedding and christening processions.
>
> "Perhaps," said Ashton-Kirk, after a moment's study of the prospect, "yes, perhaps it **is** a hole of a place in which to live. but you see we've had this house since shortly after the Revolution; four generations have been born here. As I have no fashionable wife and I live alone, I am content to stay. The house suits me; everything is arranged to my taste."[5]

So much for the rigors of the Melting Pot.

Within this ethnic wilderness, Ashton-Kirk dwells as serene as a jewel in a toad's head. All stories of the house are filled with that polished perfection found mainly in magazines. In one respect, this house differs from other glassy jewels of cultivated living: it is entirely abrim with books. Books, pamphlets, folios, rare, desired, unobtainable. Mr. Ashton-Kirk is an unrestrained bibliophile, long before Lord Peter Wimsey took up the hobby. He is bullish on American first editions, books on crime, special editions of almost anything.

His conversation reflects these interests. As the smoke of fine cigars coils up, Ashton-Kirk natters brightly of literary matters, of writers and books and special press runs. Of Stevenson and DeQuincy, and Dostoyeffsky [sic], and that naughty Benvenuto Cellini.

While he revels in his hobby, a fairly substantial household buzzes around him. There seem to be no female servants. But there is a grave-faced German Butler named Stumph, and the cook Edouard. And somewhere below you may find Dixon, the chauffeur, who threads Ashton-Kirk's big French car among the push carts outside.

The remaining staff is less conventional. It includes a dapper young man named Fuller, brisk, boyish, and infallible, who seems to be a combination secretary and chief investigator. On command, Fuller materializes, hands filled with sheets of typewritten data, whenever Ashton-Kirk feels the need for data.

Since every mystery requires endless probing, Fuller does all the legwork, all the boring research, all the drab labor. He is aided by a nest of others--Burgess, Neill, Purvis are named; others float anonymously, waiting for the call to action.

Apparently Ashton-Kirk employs all these people, every one, as his investigative arm, a cadre of full-time investigators to support his casual dips into detection. How strange.

Ashton-Kirk is officially nothing, a book collector, not a professional detective. There he lounges in his slum, his long, supple fingers controlling hordes of expensive investigators. When he speaks, they bound. At once.

Who they are, where they come from, what they do outside the novels--these matters are delicately left unresolved. It is absolutely amazing. It is like a piece of fiction.

As is Ashton-Kirk's relationship with the police.

He is the golden boy down at police headquarters. He's done them favors, he has, and they beam on him. Granted, it might please them to see him fall on his nose once in a while. Not that he ever does. When he succeeds, they get the credit, he gets the fun. It is the perfect symbiosis. The beat cops know him. So do the detectives and the higher-ups in administration. Let him ask that a man be held, or a man be released, and, lo, it is done. He wanders about crime scenes, picking up clues and putting them down. He confers with the officer in charge--no secrets between them. And when he needs a strong force of the boys in blue, they come racing to his call, eager as pups.

It's the same nice relationship that Nick Carter had with the police. Since then, if we are to believe Ed McBain, things have changed. But back then....

Here is Ashton-Kirk, unexpectedly showing up at the murder scene:

    Detective Osburne: "Why, hello. You're the last person I was looking for. How did you hear about this?"

    Ashton-Kirk: "I got it in an unusual sort of way, and came down to have a look.... May we go up?" [He has a friend with him.]

    Osburne: "Sure. Only don't pull things around any. That young fellow they've elected coroner is awful touchy about such things. He wants to be the first always." [As shown in the books, the coroner does all the investigation, just as on television, while the police stand nodding sagely.]

Ashton-Kirk: "Nothing of importance shall be disturbed."[6]

You must admit that Osburne is obliging enough. But then he recognizes that Ashton-Kirk is a gentleman--and gentlemen may be trusted not to tumble the clues about or carry sackfulls of them away. Not real gentlemen. For such valid reasons, the police trust Ashton-Kirk utterly.

As do representatives of the Treasury Department, the Secret Service, and, for that matter, the State Department. All agencies sprain themselves to accommodate his whims. For when you are wealthy and of good family, people are naturally friendly.

So the general background against which subsequent novels flash.

According to a note in **Ashton-Kirk Investigator**, the next book in the series was to be titled **Ashton-Kirk and the Scarlet Scapular** ("in press"). But somehow there was a delay. That title never appeared and readers, fretful and pallid, faced two years of silence before publication of **Ashton-Kirk Secret Agent** in 1912. This book propels Ashton-Kirk gracefully into the world of international intrigue, the spy world. Called, in 1912, the world of the diplomatic agent.

The diplomatic agent was more than a spy. He was a high-level trouble shooter, secretly laboring in the national interest. Back then, it was easier to define national interest. The diplomatic agent schemed and plotted behind his public identity. Sometimes he hit people on the head or carried them off, tied and miserable. Not good people, you understand. Scoundrels only--other nations' diplomatic agents opposing us, the fools.

In 1912, the diplomatic agent was all the fad. The Oppenheim novels of intrigue spilled out. In the **Popular Magazine,** George Bronson-Howard had introduced that smooth little fashion-plate, Norry, who had a penchant for wrecking German plans. (He did so from 1905 to 1923.) And in the 1910 **Blue Book,** Herbert New had introduced the Diplomatic Free Lance series. This ran uninterruptedly every month until 1933, the longest of all magazine series. It featured that incredible genius, Trevor, his wife, his friends, later his incomparable children. All battled menaces from Germany, Russia, Japan, all monthly, all wicked.

You may recall that Sherlock Holmes also did his turn as a secret agent. So it is no wonder that Ashton-Kirk joined the trend. He joined all trends. When secret agents were popular, he played secret agent--as, later, he became a criminologist when those classy fellows caught the public attention.

In **Secret Agent,** you may assume that Ashton-Kirk disguised and deducted, and was obstructed by a well-meaning girl, and struggled against shrewd, ruthless men. You would be correct. Did you also guess that Ashton-Kirk's efforts prevented a deep-seated intrigue from hurling nations into conflict?

You did, eh?

Ashton-Kirk Special Detective (1914) is one of those atmospheric things occurring at a frowning old castle in Pennsylvania. Yes, Pennsylvania. Unspecified terror grips those within the battlements. Strange figures glide the black corridors. From somewhere out in the countryside, weird boomings quake the night. Strange watchers huddle and whisper, leers warping their faces. While at the inn, off behind the trees, plots smoke thickly upward, like fumes from an over-heated frying pan. It is all weird and strange.

Bat Scanlon, a close friend, calls in Ashton-Kirk to discover why fear stalks the castle. No sooner does Ashton-Kirk enter, than he leaves. For several chapters, Scanlon carries the story. Then Ashton-Kirk returns, densely disguised, to investigate the menace in the night and to speak cryptically.

Ultimately the cast gathers in the cellars spreading grimly beneath the castle--the fetid, shadowed cellars, swathed in menace, where stone floors and dripping walls breathe the scent of doom. Surely you remember those cellars?

Then the secret passage grates open. Then the criminals slither grinning forth. And as their hands clutch at the concealed prize, Ashton-Kirk's voice rings sternly out.

The dour reader may grunt at the shadow of **The Hound of the Baskervilles** looming over this novel. It's true that McIntyre has dispensed with both the hound and Doyle's narrative intensity. However he has kept enough of Doyle's story sequencing to leave the impression that a friend has got all dressed up in a stranger's clothing.

By some literary miracle, **Special Investigator** also manages to reproduce the flavor of one of those less successful Nick Carter novels--one of those where one vaguely related thing occurs after another until the requisite number of pages are filled. At which time the story drops in its tracks.

The Ashton-Kirk novels do tend to the abrupt ending. The climactic scene erupts in some histrionic locale--the grim castle basement, the dead man's rooms--splendid settings, glowering with menace. then a flurry of action. The characters leap hotly about, evil grinding its teeth at good. Then a rattle of explanations as Ashton-Kirk crisply reveals all. And up rolls the final period.

These endings owe less to the craft of the novel than to the art of the stage. They are blood relatives of the final big scene which closes a four-act melodrama. The suspense builds, the dialogue races, the action climaxes and resolves. All before the grand immobilities of the stage set. It is a form McIntyre knew well.

Certain other stage elements creep into the novels. Character parts pepper them. Each part is broadly drawn with plenty of eccentricities for an actor to bite into: the German servant, the red-faced innkeeper, the Yiddish plotter, the fashionable young man, the garrulous old countryman:

> **Countryman** (responding to a request for direction): "There's three or four ways of getting there. You can go up the pike and turn at Harbinson's store; or you can turn down the lane along there a piece and go along until you come to--"
> **Scanlon:** "Which is the nearest?"
> **Countryman:** "I ain't never passed no judgment on that; but I think the clay road down toward Plattville would get you there quickest--if you didn't get stuck in the ruts."

Character building in every line. McIntyre had listened to the cadence and usage and casual humor of everyday speech:

> "Looking up the Dago? I knowed he'd put a knife or something into somebody, someday. These people with bad

tempers ought to be chained up short."

Slangy voices cut across the bland prose, and you listen, suddenly surprised, at a living voice:

"He's lapped up a good bit of booze first and last, and sometimes he's come home pretty well settled."

Not that the Ashton-Kirk adventures make you feel that you are reading a novelized play--not in the least. You do not sense the passage of the acts as you do (for example) in the Robert Curtis novelizations of certain Edgar Wallace plays. But the sense of stage in Ashton-Kirk is strong.

After **Special Investigator,** distinct change grips the series. McIntyre seems to have tired of thinking up clues and deductions in job lots. Ashton-Kirk is quietly moved from stage center to a rather less visible position over near the wings. No longer does he shape the immediate action. The spotlight has shifted to the figure of Bat Scanlon, Ashton-Kirk's friend of the previous novel.

Scanlon is a fine, strong character. Not a deducer, he is a man of action, quick and intelligent. He is an ex-wrestling champion, an adventurer from the raw West, a former deputy marshal of Gunnison County. He is "a very big man with massive shoulders and chest...; he was about forty-five but he looked pink and swift and fit."

Like Bat Masterson and other famous westerners, Scanlon has come East to a new life. He has opened a gymnasium, oversees the training of the police department's athletic team, ministers to the physical health of the fit and unfit.

Ashton-Kirk Criminologist (1918) is told through Scanlon's eyes. Our hero, Ashton-Kirk, floats amiably about the edges of his own novel.

It is another murder puzzle. The dead man has been bashed with a bronze candlestick and the fool young man obviously did it. But now complications set in. The paralyzed girl marches about. The hard-boiled thugs plot in their sordid lair. The valuable necklace vanishes. The superb girl (who plucks Scanlon's heart) consorts with all those underworld types.

What guilty secret does she hide? And how can Scanlon reveal her actions to Ashton-Kirk's relentless intelligence. Why he might suspect her; he might fix the crime upon her. And how are you to know what Ashton-Kirk thinks. No one ever knows. As he says, "until a theory is proven beyond question, it is my rule never to outline my theories."

It's enough to tear a man apart. This superb girl is obviously guilty. Yet still....

Well, Ashton-Kirk proves that she isn't. No indeed. The least likely person is. And on this pleasing note the series ends, a hint of wedding bells for Scanlon, and the spirit of Sherlock Holmes bending over all.

The fate of an imitator is hard. History remembers Holmes but not Ashton-Kirk, remembers Baker Street and Mrs. Hudson and Watson, but not the house in the slums and Stumph and Scanlon. No doubt this is not just, for Ashton-Kirk is a thoroughly charming young man. But there have been so many detectives since 1910, so many mysteries, so many styles and fashions, all fluff at the mercy of the great cat Time.

The Ashton-Kirk books are minor amusements, hollow as a glass ball. For all their brightness, they only reflect. They show nothing new--only subjects for sure popularity, changing as the popular fancy changes. They are deft, nimble, unoriginal as a mirror, shallow as a reflection, guileless.

Defects, certainly. Defects that have been accorded history's usual punishment. For if yesterday's great detectives drowse on the bookshelf, remembered only in anthologies, yesterday's lesser figures are simply obliterated. The great cat shows no pity.

Still, we can find a few kind words for Ashton-Kirk. A book collector cannot be all bad. Within the rigor of the Holmes formula, he is a cheerful figure, vivacious and agreeably competent. Sparks of sassy humor ornament his adventures. The dialogue often prances. The lost world of the early 1900s often rises around us, rattling with life.

Minor virtues, to be sure. But still worth a reading when modern complexities have rasped you gravely and what your spirit really craves is a few hours with a young man, unruffled by difficulties, who manages, against all experience, to be forever and entirely correct.

---

1. All preceding quotations are from **Ashton Kirk Investigator,** Penn Publishing, 1910, pp. 28-30.

2. **Ashton-Kirk Criminologist,** Penn Publishing Co., 1918, p. 66.

3. After the initial publication by the Penn Publishing Company (Philadelphia), the novels were reprinted three or more times. The reprint publishers include Palmer (mid-'Teens), Robinson & Birch (1921-1922), and A.L. Burt (early 'Thirties).

4. Jacques Barzun and Wendall Hertig Taylor, **A Catalogue of Crime,** p. 301. The remark applies only to the Ashton-Kirk novels, not those about Jerry Mooney.

5. **Ashton-Kirk Investigator** (1910), pp. 19-20.

6. **Ashton-Kirk Investigator,** p. 56.

The Violent World of Mike Hammer

Jim Traylor

The possibility of violence is ever present with Mike Hammer. He exists on the edge of trouble and often forces confrontations. Early in his career, Mike establishes himself as a tough guy, one who talks tough to both murder suspects and the police. **I, the Jury** (1947) establishes a number of recurring patterns in the Hammer saga. The first occurs when Mike is questioning the homosexual couple, George Kalecki and Hal Kines. Mike is berating Kalecki, trying to force information from him, when Kines jumps the detective. It's a mistake. Hammer mauls him: "I'm three sizes bigger and a hell of a lot tougher and I'll beat the living daylights out of you if you try anything funny again." The more Mike talks to the two, the madder he gets. Soon, Kalecki makes the mistake of calling Mike a "dirty two-bit shamus," and Mike gives him a taste of the violence that Kines had received: "My fist went in up to the wrist in his stomach. He flopped to the floor vomiting his lungs out, his face gradually turning purple."

Mike's actions here seem indefensible, except that the reader soon learns that Pat Chambers has been watching the whole affair waiting to intervene. Kines and Kalecki are in the rackets, and, as far as Pat and the police are concerned, the two deserve a little rough treatment. It is also true that Mike was only physically violent after Kines jumped him from behind. Up until that point he had only been verbally abrasive.

I, the Jury also contains the first fight scene in which Mike is attacked by hoods sent to keep him from uncovering the truth about a murder. Mike is questioning Bobo Hopper in the back room of Big Sam's Hi-Ho Club in Harlem when two black guys jump him. Spillane begins the encounter in his typical mode of realism, but the fight soon takes on overtones of the surrealistic. The reader is confronted with broken wrists and noses, busted jaws, a number of bruised ribs, and the inevitable vomit. Again, Mike acts in self defense.

> The knife came out again and this time I got the hand in a wristlock and twisted. The tendons stretched, and the bones snapped sickeningly.
> There was no sense to busting my hand on his skull, so I lashed out with my foot and the toe of my shoe caught the guy right in the face. He toppled over sideways, still running, and collapsed against the wall. His lower teeth were protruding through his lip. Two of his incisors were lying beside his nose, plastered there with blood.

> The high yellow was holding his broken wrist in one hand, trying to get to his feet. I helped him. My hand hooked in his collar and dragged him up. I took the side of my free hand and smashed it across his nose. The bone shattered and blood poured out.

This is not gratuitous violence, merely a fantasy world in which one man can defend himself totally against two guys who jump him because he is getting too close to the truth about a murder. It's a description of a man capable of defending himself, written for those who do not live in such a world. The description is engrossing as realistic prose can be; but it does not present such action as the only solution to the problems of man.

Mickey Spillane's PI Mike Hammer has come to be considered the antithesis of the methodical and fair-minded detective. Furthermore, his predilection for violence has led to some of the vilest denunciations ever written by critics. However, within Spillane's fictive cosmos, such sentiment is quite over-reactive. Most of Hammer's violence is merely poetic.

Hammer has three fights with Feeney Last in **My Gun Is Quick** (1950). Two are quick and violent, the other is long and deadly. The first reestablishes Hammer's macho image and his inclination to defend the helpless. He fights Feeney because he's bullying Nancy Sanford ("Red") at a bar. He gives him a quick, hard shove to the stomach, and "he snapped shut like a jackknife." When that's not enough to keep Feeney down, Hammer pulls his .45 and tells him that if he moves he'll blow his head off. The next line is classic Spillane humor: "He moved, all right. He fainted."

At their next meeting Mike whips Feeney once more and again Spillane ends the encounter on a humorous note:

> I stood up and pulled on what remained of my new suit, then picked Feeney up and hoisted him on my shoulder. Just across from my car was a newly opened grave with a canopy up and chairs all set, waiting for a new arrival. I leaned forward and Feeney Last dropped six feet to the bottom of the grave and never moved. I hoped they'd find him before they lowered the coffin, or somebody was going to get the hell scared out of him.
> The gatekeeper came to the side of my car as I was pulling out to say a friendly word and be complimented on his handiwork. He took one look at me and froze there with his mouth open. I put the car in gear. "Mighty unfriendly corpses you have in this place," I said.

These two fights are preliminaries to the death struggle between Feeney and Hammer after Feeney has killed Lola Bergen. Hammer literally beats Feeney's brains out:

> I didn't want my gun ... just my hands. My fists were slashing into the pale oval of his face, reaching for his throat. He brought his knees up and I turned just in time and took it on my leg. He only had one hand he could use, and he chopped with it, trying to bring the side of his palm against my neck. He kicked me away, pushed with the warm, bloody mess that used to be fingers and swung again, getting me in the ear.

> Feeney tried to say "No!", but my hands had his throat, squeezing ... slamming his head to the concrete floor until he went completely limp. I rolled on top of him and took that head like a sodden rag and smashed and smashed and smashed and there was no satisfying, solid thump, but a sickening squashing sound that splashed all over me.
> Only then did I let go and look at Feeney, or what was left of him, before I got sick to my stomach.

Hammer's reaction is that of a personal revenger, the man who has seen his fiance killed and chased and caught the killer. In the heat of the moment Mike has destroyed a brutal killer in a way which seems more brutal than that used by the Evil One. However, it only seems more brutal. Spillane did not describe Lola's murder. Mike narrates every detail of Feeney Last's death. The reader knows that Feeney deserved death and has no remorse. He is proud of Mike; he identifies with his actions, even if he cannot rationally justify them.

In **Vengeance Is Mine** (1950) there are six fight scenes, one about every other chapter. Spillane varies the action by opening the novel with Hammer **not** in complete control. Chester Wheeler, another one of Mike's friends, has been murdered. In the course of his investigation, Hammer cold-cocks a bouncer at Dinky Williams' Bowery Inn (leaving him in a chair as a decoy) and shoots a guy in the leg on a dare because the guy knows Hammer has just lost his PI ticket.

Hammer's fight with Juno Reeves is the memorable scene. Just as Hammer's confrontation with Charlotte Manning climaxes **I, the Jury**, Mike's fight with Juno at the conclusion of **Vengeance Is Mine** is a classic encounter, made all the more impressive by Hammer's discovery that Juno is a transvestite:

> I forgot all my reservations about shooting a woman then. I laughed through the blood on my lips and brought the Luger up as Juno swung around with eyes blazing a hatred I'll never see again. The rod was jumping in my hand, spitting nasty little slugs that flattened the killer against the wall with periods that turned into commas as the blood welled out of the holes. Juno lived until the last shot had ripped through flesh and intestines and kicked the plaster from the wall, then died with those rich, red lips split in a snarl of pain and fearful knowledge.

One Lonely Night is perhaps the most violent of the Hammer stories. A conservative body count for Mike in this novel exceeds thirty, most of whom he machine guns in the abandoned paint warehouse where the Communists have Velda strung up naked from the rafters, trying to force her to tell where the secret microfilm is hidden:

> They heard my scream and the awful roar of the gun and the slugs tearing into bone and guts and it was the last they heard. They went down as they tried to run and felt their insides tear out and spray against the walls.
> I saw the general's head splinter into shiny wet fragments and splatter over the floor. The guy from the subway tried to stop the bullets with his hands and

dissolved into a nightmare of blue holes.

There was only the guy in the pork-pie hat who make a crazy try for a gun in his pocket. I aimed the tommy gun for the first time and took his arm off at the shoulder. It dropped on the floor next to him and I let him have a good look at it. He couldn't believe it happened. I proved it by shooting him in the belly. They were all so damned clever!

They were all so damned dead! I laughed and laughed while I put the second clip in the gun. I knew the music in my head was going wild this time, but I was laughing too hard to enjoy it. I went around the room and kicked them over on their backs and if they had faces left I made sure they didn't. I saved the last burst for the bastard who was MVD in a pork-pie hat and who looked like a kid. A college boy. He was still alive when he stared into the flame that split out of the muzzle only an inch away from his nose.

The reader cannot really tell how many people are killed here. The estimate comes from Mike's recap in **The Girl Hunters** (1962). Spillane once stated that the figure is about forty, cut down from eighty in the original manuscript by his editors at Dutton. This description presents Hammer in his closest form to Carroll John Daly's Race Williams. Together with the climactic fight scene of **The Twisted Thing** (1966), these are the two scenes most similar to the mass killings to which Williams sometimes resorted. It is also interesting to compare Daly's **Murder from the East** (1935) to **One Lonely Night**. In Daly's novel, Race Williams fights the Yellow Peril, those from the East; in Spillane's novel, Hammer fights the Red Peril, the murderous Commies who would also destroy America and the world. Both novels are certainly jingoistic, but crackerjacks as entertainment.

Also in **One Lonely Night**, Hammer had defended Velda from a punk in a bar (much as he had defended Lola's honor in a similar situation in **My Gun Is Quick**. By the standards of the machine-gun deaths at the end, it's a pretty tame affair; but it does show Hammer's way of protecting his loved ones. Velda is far from defenseless. She's thrown a drink (glass and all) in a guy's face just as Mike arrived at the bar. Mike just breaks the punk's knife and drags "the cold sharp metal of the rod across his face until he was a bright red mask mumbling for me to stop." After he's beaten the guy up, Mike walks over to Velda: "Very good," I said. "Thanks. I knew you were watching." With Velda it's a little love game, a continuation of the games Mike played with her in **I, the Jury**. If Mike cannot declare his love directly, he can show here with his actions.

There are other similarities with Race Williams. In 1922 Race told the reader: "My conscience is clear. I never shot a man who didn't deserve it." Mike never uttered such a sentence, but all his actions support it.

Still, Mike wasn't always the winner in these confrontations. In **The Big Kill** (1951) he's taken for the last ride by mobsters from Lou Grindle and Ed Teen's gang. They want to find out what he knows, then kill him. Even though he's their prisoner, he baits them:

I should have kept my mouth shut. Lou Grindle backhanded me across the mouth so that my teeth went right through my lips. Two guns hit me in the spine at the same time ramming me right into him and I couldn't have gotten away with it in a million years but I tried anyway. I hooked him down as low as I could then felt my knuckles rip open when I got him in the mouth.

Neither of the guys behind me dared risk a shot, but they did just as well. One of them brought a gun barrel around as hard as he could. There wasn't even any pain in it, just a loud click that grew into a thunderous wave of sound that threw me flat on the floor and rolled over me.

The pain didn't come until later. It wasn't there in my head where I thought it would be. It was all over, a hundred agonizing points of torture where the toe of a shoe had ripped through my clothes and torn into the skin. Something dripped slowly and steadily like a leaky faucet. Every movement sent the pain shooting up from my feet and if screaming wouldn't have only made it worse I would have screamed. I got one eye open. The other was covered by a puffy mass of flesh on my cheekbone that kept it shut.

The hoods proceed very methodically to beat the crap out of Hammer. They keep knocking him out and then reviving him with cold water until they think he'll tell them what they want to know. Ed Teen tells him he can't use the information he has if he's dead and asks for it again. Mike responds: "Tell ... me what the hell ... you want." With this reply, Teen realizes that Mike doesn't know anything and okays Mike's death. The hood named Johnny takes Mike for the last ride, but Mike distracts him long enough to grab the spare gun he keeps in the car (also a Race Williams trick): "I shot him through the head five times with the .32 I had pulled out of the boot and kicked him out in the road after I took my gun from his hand. When I backed around the lights of the car swept over him in time to catch one final involuntary twitch and Johnny was getting his first taste of hell." Mike brings this encounter to a satisfactory close by driving back to the hideout and pretending to be Johnny. In the fight that follows he tricks Grindle into killing his own man and then shoots him with a bullet which "went up through his mouth into his brain."

Mike pulls one of his most humorous tricks in **Kiss Me, Deadly** (1952). Two hoods have captured Mike and are taking him for a ride, this time in the new car that he'd been given because his roadster, containing Mike and the already dead body of Berga Torn, had been run off a cliff. Mike was so pissed afterwards that the murderer tried to placate him by sending a new car, booby trapped with **two** bombs. When Mike is picked up by the hoods, he pretends that he only found the one wired to the ignition, not the one which was supposed to go off after he had driven a set number of miles. This information scares the hood that's driving so badly that he slams on the brakes and causes his buddy in the back seat to pitch forward, giving Mike the chance he needs. The driver shoots his buddy accidentally, and Mike pushes the guy's hand back so that with his next shot he kills himself. Then Mike pulls this maneuver:

I got in the driver's side, sat the two things next to me in an upright position and drove back the way we came. I found a cutoff near the airport, turned into it and followed the road until it became a one-lane drive and when I reached its limit there was a sign that read DEAD END.

> I was real cute this time. I sat them both under the sign in a nice, natural position and drove back home.

All these examples are from the early Hammer novels (1947-1952), the ones which readers remember the best and at which the anti-Spillane critics became most irate. However, Hammer's world was fully as violent in the second phase of his career (1962-1970). **The Girl Hunters** (1962) had two vividly realized scenes, each just as effective as any in the early Spillane novels:

> Just how **did** you kill a dragon? ... I walked around ... looking for an indication. I found it on a workbench.... A twenty-penny nail and a ball peen-hammer....
> I went back and turned Comrade Gorlin over on his face.
> I stretched his arm out palm down on the floor....
> It was too bad he wasn't conscious.
> Then I held the nail in the middle of the back of his hand and slammed it in with the hammer and slammed and slammed and slammed until the head of that nail dimpled his skin.... I threw the hammer down beside him and said, "Better'n handcuffs, buddy."

Hammer's "handcuffing" of Tooth, the male member of the Dragon hit team, by nailing his hand to the floor is an appropriately violent culmination to as bloody a fight scene as Spillane ever wrote. Of course, the ending with the exploding shotgun blowing up Laura Knapp (Nail, the female member of Dragon) is just as violent as Hammer's pulling the trigger on the screaming Berin-Grotin in **My Gun Is Quick**, but it is more positive because Mike is going to a loving world:

> I said, "So long, baby."
> Then I turned and walked toward the outside and Velda and behind me I heard the unearthly roar as she pulled both triggers at once.

Of the second phase, **The Snake** (1964) is the one Hammer adventure which seems less violent than the others. The story is miniscule, somewhat confused and seems to come alive only when Hammer rescues Velda the second time, and the skeleton in the car brings an end to **The Snake**:

> [Sonny Motley] gave the door a sharp jerk.... The pull on the door was enough to rock the car and ever so steadily the corpse of Blackie Conley seemed to come to life.
> [Sonny] turned ... just enough to see the man he had killed collapse into dust fragments, and as it did the bony finger touched the trigger ... and the rifle squirted a blossom of roaring flame that took Sonny Motley square in the chest....
> The skull of Blackie Conley bounced out of the cab and rolled to a stop face to face with Sonny.

The Body Lovers (1967) and **Survival ... Zero!** (1970) were not first-class Hammer adventures, although each has its classic scene. **The Body Lovers** is best remembered for presenting Mike in a tuxedo.

The violent aspect of his world has been narrowed. He still meets other tough guys, but the physically violent beating scenes are greatly curtailed here. In fact, the destructive scene is Hammer's wiring the house of Belar Ris and Dulcie McInnes to destroy the entire cell of the members of a high-level sex club:

> That single room would be gas-packed, a monstrous potential of destruction waiting to be triggered into instant hell.
> **In my car I heard the stutter of the ringing phone.**
> Six miles away a brilliant glow ... blossomed in the sky.... There were more seconds of night-quiet, then the thunderous roar came in with its wave of shock that rattled windows of the buildings behind us.
> ... "What the hell was that!"
> "Wrong number," I said and walked to the car.

In **Survival ... Zero!** Mike has cornered Stanley, the guy who killed his war pal Lippy Sullivan. This encounter is Hammer's last recorded fight scene:

> I should have shot him and had it over with, but I didn't want it to happen that fast....
> ... I jumped him, the gun forgotten now. all I wanted to use was my hands....
> ... He was flat out under me and I was bringing his own knife up under his throat ....
> He still fought, and he was still able to see what was happening when his own hand drove the knife through his neck until it was imbedded in the floor behind.

Hammer kills three other guys in rapid order before he corners the masterminds of the germ warfare plot, William Dorn and Renee Talmage. Spillane ties together several thematic ends with this final perfidious woman. Mike tells Renee: "Shut up... For a whole lifetime I'm going to have to look back and remember that I liked you once. It's going to be a damn nasty memory as it is, so for now, just shutup."

Mike goes out with one final trick, similar to the "Dead End" joke he used in **Kiss Me, Deadly**. He cons the two Evil Ones into biting cyanide capsules. He had been threatening them with an empty gun; as soon as they bit the capsules he points the gun to his head and pulls the trigger. They're both dying and scrambling for the guns they've tossed away, wanting their last action to be Mike's death. It's Hammer's last appearance in his violent world:

> Renee had the gun in her fingers and William Dorn was trying to tear it from her when the cyanide hit them in an awful spasm.
> And I was laughing in a very quiet room.

Readers are not wrong to see violence as a key element in the world of Mike Hammer. Earlier in **Survival ... Zero!** Mike had told a then-adoring Renee Talmage: "Sometimes I kill people." This calm statement reminds one of Race Williams telling the reader that he never killed a man who didn't deserve it. In the mythic world of Mike Hammer the good must kill the evil. Even though the stories are melodramatic and seem mere comic book stories with superficial characterizations, the key point to remember with Spillane is that **the stories work.**

Spillane calls himself a mere teller of tales. One of his most famous quotes was in reaction to a severe critical lambasting: "Gee, didn't he know it was only a story?" The story is everything with Spillane. His talent lies in his ability to create a world in which the rules are different from the world that the reader knows but which are perfectly consistent. There are no false notes in Hammer's violent world if one is willing to suspend disbelief to be entertained. Just as a poet would create a world which a readers knows is not accurate but a mere state of mind, Spillane has created Hammer's world of violence. Not realizing the talent that it takes to perform such a task, many critics have fallen into the trap of denigrating Spillane. Such criticism is especially true of women critics, although male critical reaction is in general just as much anti-Spillane.

What then can be said for this most famous of literary characters? This Mike Hammer? Truly he is a unique character, much imitated by the paperback action thrillers that are the modern version of the pulp magazine. Where would Mack Bolan be without Mike Hammer as father?

It is of course not true that Spillane made the real world more violent because he exerted undue influence on an unsuspecting society. We can thank World War II and the development of mass communication for that. What we can thank Spillane for is for being a master story-teller, one who has created, if not the best hard-boiled detective, at least the one most remembered.

The Old Man in the Corner

Earl F. Bargainnier

In 1977 International Polygonics, Ltd., issued **The Man in the Corner**, a facsimile of the first American edition of a group of stories by the Baroness Emmuska Orczy, with an introduction by Burke N. Hare(!), listed as editor-in-chief of the IPL Library of Crime Classics. His assistant editors are identified as Tony and Maddalena Sparafucile, presumably descendants of the assassins in Verdi's **Rigoletto**. Whoever hare and the Sparafuciles actually are, they have intentionally or otherwise raised a bibliographical question. The question involves Dover Publications' **The Old Man in the Corner: Twelve Mysteries**, issued in 1980 with an introduction by E.F. Bleiler. When Ms. Sparafucile wrote her introduction to IPL's reprint of Orczy's **Lady Molly of Scotland Yard** (1981), she attacked the Dover volume for being "somewhat misleading" in using the title it has. She omits the fact that it clearly states "Twelve Mysteries," indicating that it makes no pretense to completeness. The introductions to both books agree that there are thirty-eight Old Man stories, but the IPL's **The Man in the Corner** (the original American title[3] tries to give the impression that it is complete, even though its thirty-six chapters contain only twelve stories, no more than the Dover volume. The IPL collection consists of the first and second series minus the repressed story, "The Glasgow Mystery," which is included in the Dover volume. Five stories are in both, thus the two volumes together provide nineteen, exactly half the presumed total.

It is unlikely that a collection of all the Old Man stories will be published anytime soon, but surely someone can provide a list of all the stories as originally published in magazine form and then in their first collected form: **The Case of Miss Elliott** (1905), six of an undetermined number in the Dover edition; **The Old Man in the Corner** (1909), the twelve in the IPL volume plus "The Glasgow Mystery"; and **Unravelled Knots** (1924-1925), an unknown number. Such a list would at least clear up the utter confusion created by the remarks in the three introductions mentioned. Both volumes of Old Man stories are welcomed by those investigating early detective fiction, but readers should not be misled by the pseudonymous Mr. Hare and Ms. Sparafucile into believing that the IPL volume is a completion of Orczy's Old Man Stories.

Aside from the bibliographical question, the stories themselves raise some intriguing critical ones. (If you have never read these stories and wish to, you should stop here, as much will be given away, **pace** Ms. Sparafucile.) First, is there any other group of stories or novels featuring a series detective in which none of the criminals are ever punished? The Old Man gives his solutions to Polly Burton, or an anonymous "I," in the Norfolk Street ABC (Aerated Bread Company) lunchroom, and only the Old Man, his listener, and the reader know the truth. No attempt is made to follow up on the cases, which remain in "the category of so-called impenetrable mysteries." the Old Man's use of "so-called" in the closing statement of "The York Mystery" indicates his amusement at knowing what the police do not, and his laughter or grins at his conclusions about other cases are further evidence. For him, crime-solving is purely intellectual puzzle; neither justice nor punishment enter into his deliberations.

Perhaps the reason is the result of a second question raised by the stories. Is there another amateur detective who has earlier been a very brutal, cold-blooded murderer for gain, one who has totally succeeded in his crime? "The Mysterious Death in Percy Street," the final story in **The Man in the Corner**, reveals such to be the case with the Old Man. Since he has escaped punishment for murder, it is not surprising that he is indifferent to the punishment of other criminals. He describes himself as murderer as "one of the most ingenious men of the age" and seems to take as much pride in having committed a murder as in having solved others. His story of his leaving his unconscious aunt, whom he has stunned, to freeze in five-below-zero weather in order to steal eight hundred pounds ends his relationship with Polly Burton on a macabre note. Certainly, it is much more shocking than Hercule Poirot's "justifiable" murder in **Curtain**, for there Poirot must also die. The Old Man just walks out of the lunchroom. (Another question: to whom does he relate the later stories? In the six stories from **The Case of Miss Elliott** included in the Dover edition, the listener is simply "I.")

The fact that the Old Man is a murderer offers an answer to the lack of any other information about him. He is old, but how old? And why did the American publisher decide to drop the **Old**? The original illustrations provide no help. Where does he live? What does he do beside knot string and eat cheesecake? Is there a family--besides the late aunt? What is his name? No such details are even hinted at, much less given. The Old Man has the desire to present his ingenuity to his awed listeners, but he obviously has no intention of endangering himself by letting them or anyone else know specifics about himself. Even his account of his murdering his aunt is presented obliquely.

Two final questions concern the Old Man's mysterious appearances and disappearances and his similarly mysterious ability to collect evidence in the cases. He can appear "like a veritable Jack-in-the-box" ("The Robbery in Phillimore Terrace") and is "gone before Polly could say another word" ("The De Genneville Peerage"). The same is true of those told to the first-person narrator: "Before I could reply he had gone" ("The Case of Miss Elliott"). It is as if he exists only to tell his stories or as if he is the wise old man of myth who melts or fades away except when his oracular pronouncements are required. The other unexplained element consists of the photographs which he slides across the lunchroom table as he presents details of his cases. How does he obtain them? He is never a part of the official investigation, and his odd appearance would seem to attract attention if he attempted to take the photographs himself. Even though in "The Fenchurch Street Mystery" he does state that "I took the snapshot," that is the only instance in the nineteen stories of any explanation of his possession of photographs of principals or places in a case--still another of the unanswered questions about the Old Man in the Corner.

Yet he remains one of the more famous early twentieth-century fictional detectives, often called "the first armchair detective." (A caveat to that title is expressed by Fred Dueren in "Was The Old Man in the Corner an Armchair Detective?" (**The Armchair Detective** 14:3 [Summer 1981], 232-233). Nevertheless, probably only a very few people have read all of Orczy's stories about him. the almost total lack of availability until the two collections of the past five years is undoubtedly the reason, and, as already noted, they have supplied just half of the stories. This enigmatic knotter of strings, solver of crimes, **and murderer** remains a mystery himself--both in the unanswered questions posed by the stories and in his high position among fictional detectives in spite of many of his cases being little read because they are so difficult to find.

C.B. Greenfield: The Metaphor Is the Man

Jane S. Bakerman

Americans, we are often told, enjoy--or suffer from--a frontier mentality. For about a literary generation, now, some of the most prominent American writers of crime fiction have claimed as their provinces the dark underside of that frontier mentality. Ross Macdonald and Margaret Millar, for instance, have undertaken serious examinations of California, the last frontier, and discussed the social and ecological depredations our culture has imposed upon an area which often seems Edenic on its social and geographic surface. Robert B. Parker confronts the social frontier feminism has imposed upon modern American culture; William X. Kienzle discusses changes in Roman Catholicism and describes their impact in his crime stories, and John D. MacDonald and Lawrence Sanders regularly decry selfishness and the lust for power as benchmarks of Americans' "frontier" ethics.

More recently, these commentators have been joined by yet another competent social critic, Lucille Kallen, whose emerging detective series, laced with humor, entertains while it instructs. Kallen has staked a literary claim to the little town of Sloan's Ford, Connecticut, a community which initially seems, to the armchair traveller journeying there with her, the epitome of safe suburbia, one of the last havens of both traditional American standards and the traditional American family.

However, even the most casual reading of the series, which includes, to date, three novels--**Introducing C.B. Greenfield** (1979) [subsequent page references are to the 1980 Ballantine edition], **C.B. Greenfield: The Tanglewood Murder** (Wyndham Books, 1980), and **C.B. Greenfield: No Lady in the House** (Wyndham Books, 1982)--reveals that the pleasant little town is really a microcosm of the American scene, a grim new frontier of American culture, where murder and other violence intrude with a certain regularity. After a series of robberies, for instance, narrator Maggie Rome reflects:

> Pulse pounding, I carried the groceries to the front door and inserted the key. And stopped, realizing that the comforting British expression, "safe as houses," had become obsolete. Houses were no longer safe. Not even here, forty miles from urban rot, on a peaceful, upper-middle-class suburban street inhabited by relatively decent, family-oriented, sensible people who bought season tickets to the opera and the ballet and discussed the editorials in **The Times** at their dinner parties, a street of well-cared-for lawns and excellent garbage pickup, of dogwood trees and healthy kids on bicycles. There were

no longer any safe houses here. [p. 51]

   Maggie's observation is a surprise to almost no one--the evening news and, as noted, even our recreational reading have long since conditioned us to this awareness, even if personal experience has not. But the Greenfield series also offers some comfort and hope--and therein lies much of its appeal. Further, close reading of the novels reveals that Kallen displays such competence in bringing off the somewhat intricate structure of her commentaries that their form underscores the reassurance even as the style and symbolism, market by wit, humor, and a marvelous array of allusion, **both** underscore **and** undercut the comfort quotient. The result of this dichotomy is one almost perfect pattern of detective story as social criticism: a blend of entertainment, escapism, irony, and realism. This combination of effect is difficult to achieve, but Kallen does achieve it regularly. No small feat.
   Two of the elements of comfort and hope are obvious and traditional; Kallen's amateur sleuths restore order to their suburban world which has been disordered by crime; this pattern accounts for much of the appeal of all mystery fiction. Further, Kallen's tales are clever and funny, and the humor provides comic relief from the horrors which generate the plots. Abundant literary allusion (a device not at all uncommon in mystery fiction--witness such authors as Ruth Rendell and Nicholas Freeling, for example) is used here in telling fashion. It serves to link the sometimes terrifying moments of Kallen's fictional present to a past which we choose to believe was more orderly and peaceful; and, of course, it helps enormously in characterization, particularly of her narrator-protagonist, Maggie Rome, a part-time journalist, and Maggie's co-investigator and employer, C.B. Greenfield.
   Also, the viability of the Rome-Greenfield association, their "firmly established relationship" which consists "of equal parts of comfortable friendship, grudging respect, and simple exasperation" [**Tanglewood**, p. 18], is yet another comfort to readers. While admirable and realistic characters can sustain a friendship in the face of murder, the most terrible social ill, all cannot be lost; in bonding lies hope. Hope lies also, of course, in the fact that ordinary people (people like us, the readers) can take arms against seas of troubles and, at least temporarily, end them. Decent people taking unified action reassures us that order may be achievable, despite all the evidence of the evening news or personal observation.
   Yet even in the midst of hope, irony intrudes, for Greenfield, the novels' central symbol of order and traditionalism, is also the source of much of the humor in the books. We smile--or laugh--at Greenfield, even as we long for his success. In this duality of perception lie irony, realism, fictional power. C.B. Greenfield is a contemporary knight fighting the everlasting battle on the ultimate frontier: the encroachment of evil and social decay--he is admirable, and that is comforting; he is also silly, and that is disquieting.
   The three Kallen novels to date show increasing use of violence as trigger for plot. **Introducing C.B. Greenfield**, the initial Rome-Greenfield foray into detection, recounts their search for a hit-and-run driver who has struck down a child. **C.B. Greenfield: The Tanglewood Murder** finds the pair temporarily leaving Sloan's Ford for a "music vacation," a period marred by the murder of a member of the Boston Symphony Orchestra. In **C.B. Greenfield: No Lady in the House**, the grimmest of the three novels, two Sloan's Ford women are killed; the first death occurs in Greenfield's home, and thus he feels responsible for finding the killer.

One basic motive pertains for all the crimes in the Kallen books, and this motive, heedless selfishness, becomes both theme for Kallen's social criticism and symbol for the decay of modern American culture:

> What's the essential difference between the young apes who smash beer bottles all over the parking lot, leaving it strewn with glass, and the--the hyenas who dump toxic chemicals by the roadside where children play? They're both sick with the same disease, immediate personal need. The need for gratification, or the need for financial gain, at the cost of others. The need to survive at the expense of others. How else do you explain the technological and--and scientific geniuses who justify making the water we drink unsafe, the food we eat ultimately deadly, the air we breathe finally fatal? [**Tanglewood**, p. 135]

Each of the criminals stalked by Rome and Greenfield shares this need for instant gratification, the inability to value anyone's desires but his own--lust, pride, ambition are the secondary motivations, and all amount to utter selfishness, complete irresponsibility. In this way, Kallen's villains become metaphors for the destructiveness of a selfish society, going its heedless way despite warnings and danger.

Greenfield, of course, is an issuer of many of the warnings. The owner-editor of the weekly **Sloan's Ford Reporter**, he is willing to forego advertising fees from businesspeople whose practices he despises; he campaigns for decent schools; he joins the constant outcry over cheap, fruitless pothole repair, and, even more importantly, he is willing to risk position and reputation to defeat crime and corruption. Even though he believes that

> Monstrous behavior is the order of the day. I'll tell you when to be shocked. When something human and decent happens!

Greenfield is incapable of simply standing by and thus endorsing the status quo. Instead, he feels responsible; in fact, **his** abiding need **is** the assumption of responsibility, as Maggie notes: "I was about to reply that it was her own silly tongue that had landed her in this mess, but it was useless to point that out. He **wanted** to be responsible." [**Introducing**, p. 128] Here Kallen must be very careful indeed lest her hero emerge as nothing more than a meddling demagogue who thinks that no one but himself has decent standards, and the humor serves her well in this effort. Maggie, for example, wonders whether Greenfield's penchant for involvement, for his personal assumption of social responsibility, might not have its roots partly in "a middle-aged-male syndrome: a wistful return to the sensation of being violently engaged." [**Introducing**, 107] It is Maggie's observation also that Greenfield's abandonment of a good job with NBC News in order to become "the soft-spoken gadfly of Sloan's Ford" [**Tanglewood**, p. 11] might be indulgence of "his romantic image of himself as ... king of the **Sloan's Ford Reporter**, with which he intended to vanquish corruption, greed, injustice, disease, and inferior English teachers in the school system." [**Introducing**, p. 2] Because Kallen and Maggie, her narrator, take into account the very human possibility of mixed motives on the part of the detective-hero, readers accept him even though they laugh at him.

Furthermore, Greenfield sometimes examines his own

motivation. After a verbal duel with Maggie, who is keenly upset by one of the murders, Greenfield admits: "I'm not significantly more tranquil than you. Same cause, different symptoms. Person or persons unknown invaded my house, helped themselves to my property, and murdered a girl who was working for me. I'm suffering a typical reaction of impotent rage. The rage is acceptable, the impotence is not." [**Lady**, p. 54] Romantic gadfly though he may be, Greenfield is also a thinking human being, and his unwillingness to allow evil to go unchallenged combines with Maggie's friendly doubt over the purity of his motives to win readers' approval. They quickly recognize that "something human and decent" is happening when Greenfield makes himself responsible for achieving justice. Readers see him as a fitting metaphor for traditional values, for order in an increasingly disorderly world.

This softening of Greenfield's nobility by use of humor is the easiest and the most obvious usage of comedy as Kallen's central literary device. She is on much more difficult ground when she moves into more important, more sophisticated employment of that device: when she makes Greenfield a flawed symbol of tradition and order. Among the most useful methods of developing this irony is Maggie's frequent use of antithesis. Readers' first glimpse of the editor-detective provides the only lengthy, detailed description they are given. The passage sets the pattern for Maggie's comments about her employer:

> He swiveled slowly around ... and regarded me from behind his large horn-rimmed glasses. He was a long, slope-shouldered, mournful-looking man, with wispy gray hair and the face of a dignified basset hound. His movements were supremely deliberate and his pronouncements infinitely calculated; he moved through life like a man who found himself crossing a gorge on a high wire without a net. His expression suggested he was resigned to this unaccountable infamy of fate, but ... the expression of benign and gentle melancholy was totally deceptive. He had been known to cut an ego to ribbons while giving a perfect impersonation of a kindly old country doctor handing out lollipops. [**Introducing**, p. 5]

Here, the characterization is fair and valid; Greenfield is a benign influence in the community. He is also, as dozens of episodes reveal, capable of wielding the sharpest tongue in the East, just as he is capable of isolating himself from even the most reasonable of appeals: "He had pulled up his mental drawbridge and there was no way over the moat" [**Tanglewood**, p. 82] But both Maggie and readers recognize that Greenfield's slashing tongue and stubborn deafness usually demolish people who are, in his judgment, behaving stupidly or obstructively.

It is Maggie, no gentle-tongued soul herself, who is most often the butt of Greenfield's sarcasm and of his willful manipulation of others. He forces her to do the legwork for their investigations; he never lets her forget that he is employer, that she is employee. But it is also **Maggie** who tells us these stories, and, if she sometimes grows furious with his ego, Maggie also credits (and admires) Greenfield's strengths. Again, antithesis is the telling device: "Humility was not one of Greenfield's salient characteristics; he never questioned his ability to tackle problems of inordinate size and complexity .... Instruct the UN? **Any** day. Hang a curtain? Forget it. On the other hand, his moral sense was unerring." [**Tanglewood**, p. 91]

Despite the genuine worth of Greenfield's moral sense, however, his attitudes sometimes come perilously close to childishness. Equating the old and the established with goodness and quality,

> He attached himself to products and nothing would he attached himself to products and nothing would separate him from them but termination of their manufacture. Palmolive was the only soap. Parker 51 fountain pen was the only writing instrument. When Betty Crocker's Date Bar Mix unaccountably disappeared forever from the shelves he was inconsolable for a year. Helen Deutch [another employee at the newspaper], whom he had conscripted to bake them weekly after she'd once thoughtlessly brought them to the office, tried thirty-seven substitutes to no avail. [**Tanglewood**, p. 100].

For Greenfield, panic ensues when he cannot find a bottle of Cutter's, his favorite--his **only**--brand of insect repellent; he will be neither consoled nor persuaded by Maggie's assurances that other effective products are readily available on the market. When, finally, Greenfield does locate some Cutter's, he buys a dozen bottles: "It's not inconceivable ... that the idiots will stop manufacturing it." [**Tanglewood**, p. 191] In such small, humorous details does Kallen embed the irony into her humorous portrait of Greenfield.

At one point, Maggie, discouraged and frightened by a local crime wave, falls more deeply into distress while listening to the radio which "continued its matter-of-fact litany of sudden death in the same neutral voice in which it announced the traffic conditions. No one listens, I thought. The stopper may be unplugged and intelligent life on earth slowly gurgling down the drain; nobody hears it. Preoccupation? Defense mechanism? Or simple stupidity?" [**Lady**, p. 60]

So far, of course, Greenfield, that stubborn, clever man who listens only to what he feels should be heard, **does** hear, **does** care, **does** heed, and **does** take action, sweeping Maggie along in his train. But careful readers do not forget the Cutter's, even as they laugh at Greenfield's obstinacy--at some point in the future, those "idiots" **may** stop manufacturing it, and at some further point, the last of the dozen bottles be empty and irreplaceable. Disruptive change may well occur, despite Greenfield's preventive measures, and therein lies one frightening irony of the Greenfield metaphor--traditional values may win small battles but lose the war. Cutter's, then, serves as a humorous mode of characterization and a clever, light symbol of disruptive change.

Even more importantly, however, it is also a clue to the weakness of Greenfield's character. Because he equates change with deterioration, Greenfield willingly accepts the responsibility to resist shifting standards. His willingness to fight **minor** battles (such as those waged against manufacturers' infatuation with product obsolescence) as well as **major** battles against crime and destruction attracts even as it repels. A modern Don Quixote, Greenfield is both noble **and** foolish as he wages war against selfishness, destruction, and change.

The underlying irony of Lucille Kallen's humorous portrait of a prickly but determined hero adds a good measure of cautionary realism to her comic novels. Greenfield's refusal to differentiate between the importance of his various battles against change warns readers that eccentric rigidity can be foolhardy. In contrast, his trustworthy moral sense and the actions it motivates demand that attention must be paid, that defenses against the "me generation's" selfish frontier must be mounted. The sometimes arrogant egoism of her hero, a man dedicated to warfare **against** vicious and destructive egoism is Kallen's final irony.

In these three novels, C.B. Greenfield serves as both character and metaphor. As the embodiment of both the worth and the eccentricity of unilateral traditionalism, Greenfield instructs as he entertains. His simplistic adherence to established, traditional values makes readers laugh--and resolve to avoid tenacity for tenacity's sake. His dedication to honor and the worth of the individual excites admiration--and a resolve to support Greenfield's more important commitments. In these ways, Kallen suggests to her readers that they choose their battles carefully, spending energy on the crucial causes, resisting only truly important, damaging changes.

By amusing as she criticizes, Lucille Kallen makes serious and potentially effective social comments and gives clear evidence that her relatively young series of comic crime novels belongs in the first rank of the genre. Her treatment of the dark underside of the frontier mentality is deft and thoughtful. She seems destined for prominence in her field, and she deserves it.

[1] Because of these characteristics and behaviors, C.B. Greenfield is often compared to Rex Stout's creation, Nero Wolfe. To a limited degree, this comparison is valid; the two share many traits, several methods. Greenfield, however, is an important symbol as well as an important character in the Kallen series, and in this way serves many different purposes in the novels' structure; Wolfe, on the other hand, is simply (though wonderfully effectively) the central character in the Stout novels.

VERDICTS Book Reviews

Robert Sampson. **Yesterday's Faces—Volume I: Glory Figures.** Bowling Green University Popular Press, 1983, $20.95 cloth, $10.95 paper.

This is the first volume in an ambitious series that will trace the development of series characters in the Pulps. The author, Robert Sampson, is certainly no stranger to readers of TMF, and he is regarded, with good reason, as one of the leading writers on the Pulps, their characters, and their history. No one sums up the emotional impact of the whole Pulp experience quiet as well as Sampson.

Glory Figures covers the many different series featured in dime novels and pulp magazines from the late nineteenth century until approximately 1920 and also gives an overview of the entire Pulp era. There's a great deal to interest mystery fans here.

After recapping the origins of the dime novel, Sampson examines the phenomenon of the original Nick Carter and the multitude of adventures in which he appeared. He has obviously read extensively in this series and presents a very good look at its development. I would have appreciated more information about the authors of the stories, but, understandably, that's hard to come by at this late date.

Sampson then moves on to a chapter dealing with A.J. Raffles, Arsene Lupin, Hamilton Cleek, and the Lone Wolf. This look at Rogues and Bent Heroes, as Sampson calls them, leads into an examination of Frank L. Packard's creation, Jimmie Dale, "Alias the Gray Seal." I've never been particularly fond of Packard's work, but Sampson may force me to give him another try. Anyone who can be cited as an influence on Norvell Page's wonderful **Spider** prose can't be all bad.

Edgar Wallace is the last mystery writer touched on by Sampson in this volume, in a lengthy chapter on the career of the Four Just Men. Again, Sampson has described their exploits with such flare that I'm inclined to want to read the books.

Sampson doesn't limit himself to mystery; he also covers some of the Western heroes who sprang to live during this time, and he touches on early, early science fiction characters as well. (Though science fiction series characters will be one of the focuses of the next volume, along with scientific investigators and occult detectives.)

This is a highly readable book, packed with information about stories and characters that have faded with the passage of years. Sampson brings them back in crisp, entertaining prose. We can hope that the other three volumes in this series won't be long in coming. Highly recommended. (James M. Reasoner)

Richard Ellington. **Shoot the Works.** Morrow, 1948 [Pocket, 1949].

As a fan of hardboiled private eye novels, I'm always on the lookout for a writer I haven't yet encountered. I had heard of Richard Ellington before but had never read any of his books until this one. Steve Drake, Ellington's PI-narrator, is a typical down-on-his-luck, World War II vet, tough-but-honest private eye. He operates in New York and has a tendency to be a little to descriptive about the snowy Christmas season during which **Shoot the Works** takes place. Drake, who like author Ellington has some acting experience in his background, is hired by a Park Avenue psychiatrist to keep an eye on one of the doctor's patients. The patient is a young woman, the niece of a prominent man, and she also happens to be a kleptomaniac. Drake's client is purposely vague about things, but the threat of blackmail seems to be lurking in the background.

Of course, there's a lot more lurking in the background. As Drake works his way deeper into the case, he discovers an old suicide (or was it murder?), a little insanity, a lot of covering up, and three more murders. With Drake's own life on the line, he follows the trail to Florida and finally unravels the complicated plot.

There's little in this novel that hasn't been done many times before and since, but Ellington handles it fairly well. The characters and dialogue are well done, but the outcome is very predictable and the plot is cluttered by too many characters stumbling in and out of the murder scenes too close together. **Shoot the Works** is enjoyable but not memorable, a good night's reading but nothing more. (James M. Reasoner)

Ted Wood. **Dead in the Water.** Scribner's, 1983, $11.95.

Dead in the Water is a small-town police procedural set in a Canadian lake resort area. It's also the winner of the Scribner's Crime Novel Award and the recipient of some heavy-weight advance praise. Happily, both seem to be justified.

The narrator of the novel is Reid Bennett, now the police chief of Murphy's Harbour, formerly a detective on the Toronto force who was pressured out of the apartment after using deadly force to put a stop to a gang rape in progress. Now he is a one-man force and wants basically to be left alone so that he can forget the past (or brood about it; Bennett does seem obsessed with violence and its consequences). Predictably, though, crime does crop up in Murphy's Harbour and Bennett is forced to cope with a veritable invasion of his adopted town by professional killers. He copes quite well, though his image of himself as a loner is refuted by the fact that he has to have help from his German Shepard partner, Sam, and several of the locals.

The plot of **Dead in the Water** is a standard one; the final revelations don't come as much of a surprise. But the appeal of the novel comes from other sources. Bennett is a very good character, prickly enough to be human, admirable enough to function as a hero. His relationship with the dog Sam is particularly well-drawn. Wood's prose is clean and very fast; the understated action scenes are excellent. This reads very much like the first book in a series, and I hope it is. I'd like to be able to return to Murphy's Harbour from time to time. (James M. Reasoner)

Ken Darby. **The Brownstone House of Nero Wolfe.** Little, Brown, 1983, 178 pp., $14.95.

The Brownstone House does for Nero Wolfe what William Baring-Gould's **Sherlock Holmes of Baker Street** did for the master sleuth. Namely, it tells everything you could possibly want to know about that famous residence on West 35th Street.

Ken Darby uses Archie Goodwin (now married to Lily Rowan and living in Montana) as his mouthpiece. Goodwin explains a lot of the apparently contradictory statements he made concerning the environs of Nero Wolfe throughout the seventy stories that comprise the Wolfe Canon. Did you know that the address was given as being ten different numbers, two in one story alone? That and other burning questions of Wolfe trivia are answered in this volume.

I must admit that Darby has done his homework. I would guess that every piece of conflicting information that Rex Stout included in his oeuvrer is glibly explained away by the wise-cracking archie, who seems to have just too much information (all documented!) at his aged fingertips.

This book suffers from indecisiveness. Is it a scholarly treatise or a tongue-in-cheek parody? It should have been one or the other, for the combination just doesn't come off. (Alan S. Mosier)

Ken Darby. **The Brownstone House of Nero Wolfe.** Little, Brown, 1983, 178 pp., $14.95.

I would like to think that I am about as thoroughly steeped in the minutiae of Wolfean lore as anyone. However, one thing I've never managed to get entirely straight is the layout of the brownstone, particularly the office (though I've never been confused as to which side of the hall the office is on, unlike a noted Wolfean of our mutual acquaintance). Thus this book's promise of providing a definitive guide to the house made it a must-have for me (and presumably for most Stout aficionados).

Darby does succeed in sorting out the geography of the house. The heart of the book is a set of blueprints: a lot plan, the plant rooms (2 versions), second and third floors, basement, ground floor, and, finally, the office. The blueprints are detailed and plausible, clearly the result of extensive research in the Wolfe canon. I noted only one obvious omission--Darby failed to provide room for the elevator mechanism (it belongs in a space marked "closet" on the basement blueprint). No doubt other Wolfe fans who have paid closer attention to the house and furnishing problem than I have will find many details to quarrel with. At last given a way out of my difficulty in visualizing the layout of the house, and particularly the arrangement of Wolfe's desk, Archie's desk, and the red chair, I'm willing, for now, to accept Darby's diagrams as definitive. Subject, of course, to frequent checking against the text. (And, now that I look at the office plan again, I'm a bit dubious about the placement of the wastebasket. Seems an awfully long toss for Cramer's cigars. Yes, I know, he always missed.)

That's what's good, valuable, even admirable about Darby's book. Eight pages of blueprints. The other 170 pages are quite another matter. Many of you are probably already aware of the book's premise. Wolfe has retired and is living in his house in Egypt. Archie has married Lily and is living on her ranch in Montana. (An aside here. Am I the only one who thinks Archie would be better off married to Lucy Valdon, not Lily Rowan?) It is Archie who conducts the tour of the brownstone. I.e., the text is by Archie. Or so we're supposed to believe.

Put simply, Darby's attempt to impersonate Archie Goodwin, to write in Archie's narrative style, is disastrous. It is clear after only a few pages that Darby (a Hollywood TV composer, of all things) is no stylist of any particular distinction. For him to attempt to mimic the inimitable Stout/Goodwin style is evidence of either arrogance, or stupidity, or both. Though Archie's style is, looked at superficially, unremarkable and therefore readily imitated, it is anything but. I would maintain that constructing an acceptable pastiche of Stout's Goodwin style would be a monumentally difficult task, one which even a master of pastiche would approach with fear and trembling. I can't dissect Darby's pathetic attempt at impersonating Archie, but I can tell you that virtually every sentence rings wrong, wrong, wrong. I would imagine that any Stout reader of reasonable intelligence and sensitivity would be left with the same impression. There is a naturalness and simplicity to Archie's prose that is, of course, traceable to Stout's natural facility as a writer. By all accounts, the text just flowed right out of Stout's head and onto the page, and thus Archie's character and mode of expression are inextricably connected to Stout's. Julian Symons' attempt to "do" Archie in **The Great Detectives**, while hardly a triumph, was at least palatable, and incomparably more successful than Darby's. But at least Symons had the sense not to try to write as Archie, but only to "interview" him. Darby, hardly in Symons' class as a prose stylist (he's more at the level of, say, R.A.J. Walling), clearly lacks any sense of the difficulty in attempting an acceptable pastiche.

Darby's ersatz Archie can at least be borne through the first two thirds of the book, as we tour the house and work through the floor plans. Most of the text is not fake Archie, but **real** Archie--quotations from the stories concerning the house and its layout. Darby is fairly clever in reconciling the inevitable conflicting statements as to the layout of the brownstone, and he builds a reasonably good case for his construction of the house's innards. The quotations are not exhaustive, however, so I can't state whether Darby managed to finesse some of the stickier points of architecture by simply omitting particular passages which would throw his floor plans into disarray. Still, one is at least half-willing to suspend one's displeasure with Darby's lame Archie imitation while captivated by the nifty drawings. As I said at the outset, Darby's conception of the brownstone is quite convincing (and he rightly takes a shot at Baring-Gould's half-assed attempt). But I found it convincing because it seems right to me; looks right to this Stout fanatic, who carries so much Wolfean lore in his head. I am certainly **not** convinced because "Archie" is conducting me on a tour, since this Archie is clearly an imposter.

Had Darby any sense (as we've seen, he hasn't), he would have quit when the tour of the house was completed. Instead, he really goes off the rails for several more chapters. Clearly infatuated with the notion of having an opportunity to play Archie Goodwin before an audience, he blithely continues, regaling us with an account of his life in Montana, subjecting us to countless horrors, including an excruciatingly embarrassing and utterly false romantic interlude between Archie and Lily which is guaranteed to send Stout fans on the run for the barf bags.

And it gets worse. Unimaginably worse. Not content to play Archie, Darby decides to play Wolfe as well, via a couple of "letters from Nero." Upon reflection, I think you would agree that, being a much gaudier, more theatrical character, Wolfe would be rather easier to imitate successfully than Archie. Need I bother to state that Darby's Wolfe is every bit as phony, wrong, and unconvincing as his Archie? And that's not the worst of it. Again, having a captive audience of readers, Darby takes advantage of the opportunity to enlighten us as to his views on current issues of the day, in the guise, remember, of Nero Wolfe. Since no rational being would waste time reading, let alone spend $14.95 for a book of polemic from such an obviously incandescent asshole as Ken Darby, this subterfuge is his only hope of getting his views in print.

This is **despicable**. As it happens, I am more or less in agreement with Darby's observations (the topics are, in case you're interested--and I hope by now you are not--school busing and gay lib), but that's beside the point. As Great Characters of fiction, I suppose Nero Wolfe and Archie Goodwin will inevitably be subjects for parody and pastiche. I imagine there's much more to come (one prays, not from Ken Darby), and perhaps some of them will be entertaining and a few, likely **very** few, "satisfactory" addenda to Stout's achievement. But it's one thing to appropriate such great characters for the purposes of entertainment, and homage, and quite another to utilize them for polemical diatribe. Only Rex Stout had the right to adopt the role of Archie or Wolfe to voice controversial opinions on issues of the day. I admit that I always squirm a bit on those occasions when, for instance, Wolfe would put in a plug for world government, but Stout had every right to utilize his character as his mouthpiece. That he used his characters infrequently in such roles is tribute to Stout's good sense (sense which has deserted so many writers, e.g. JDM), and contributes to the timeless quality of the Wolfe stories (and will help to assure their immortality).

Darby's sleazy appropriation of Stout's characters for the purpose of spouting off is monumentally offensive. The whole final third of the book is irrelevant to the tour of the brownstone; the "letters from Nero" irrelevant to anything having to do with the premise. Darby's **arrogance** in presenting this garbage to public view is beyond belief. Even the most casual Stout reader couldn't fail to note how this material clashes with the rest of the book, how egregious and inappropriate it all is. Where were the editors at Little, Brown? How in heaven did the Stout estate let this crap reach print? What in the world possessed John McAleer to provide jacket endorsement for this offensive abomination?

This could have been a wonderful book. Darby's research and blueprints could have been utilized as the core material of a coffee table book which would delight every Stout fan. For example, the blueprints could have been supplemented with artist's renderings of the house, the interiors, and the furnishings. Set drawings and stills from the Thayer David movie and the William Conrad TV series could have been acquired and used as well, with appropriate comment as to how those conceptions of the brownstone deviated from Darby's version. I can think of a dozen ways in which a Nero Wolfe's Brownstone Book could have been done acceptably, even brilliantly. I was anticipating something of the sort in this book. Never in my wildest nightmares would I have imagined that any Stout fan (I like to think of Wolfean folk as being people of taste and intelligence) could produce a book about the brownstone as vile as this. Let alone that any allegedly reputable publisher would let it see print.

Nero Wolfe, **the real** Nero Wolfe, ought to have the last word here, and I quote: "This is grotesque." (Art Scott)

Tage la Cour and Harald Mogensen. **Kriminallitteraturens Kavalkade: Kriminal- og detektivhistorien i billeder og tekst.** Copenhagen: Lademann, 1983.

The problem with coffee-table books is that they are coffee-table books, and some people don't like coffee-table books. Personally, I find them at best temporarily diverting, then mildly irritating. Such being the case, I am probably not the right person to review the new **Kavalkade**, but I shall try to be fair.

The original la Cour-Mogensen, **The Murder Book** in an anonymous English translation, was a pretty good job within the limitations of the form. The illustrations went beyond the old chestnuts, and the authors obviously took pains to plan their book themselves, and did not leave it to a picture researcher and a packager. I didn't like the point of the book particularly, but that is a matter of personal taste.

Now a new la Cour-Mogensen is on hand, apparently waiting for an English-language edition. It may have difficulties in crossing the ocean, for I believe that the first edition was not too successful commercially. I picked up my own copy as a remainder for $3.50 or so. But what is the new book? In the preface the authors say that it should not be considered just a second edition of **The Murder Book**. Well, it seems to me that you can describe the book honestly in two different ways, neither of which will help its sales. You can call it a new book that cannibalizes the old book very extensively, or you can say that it is a revised edition of the old book with much new material. This ambiguity will not help the book in any way.

The overall plan is the same for both books: topical segments, roughly in chronological order, with lots of colored illustrations and snippets of text often focused on the pictures. Many topics carry over from the first volume, but there are topics that have been dropped and topics that have been added. Many illustrations have been changed, and the copy is mostly new. The two books are roughly the same size. To my mind the changes have not always been made wisely. With Baroness Orczy, for example, where Lady Molly (who is not important) is retained, the more important Old Man in the Corner has been banished to a sketch.

The general tendency of the changes has been enlarging the emphasis on thrillers and procedurals, particularly very modern stuff, at the expense of other types of mystery-detection. This sometimes results in very odd proportions: four pages to Simenon; four pages to Le Carre; two pages to Mickey Spillane; two **lines** to Ruth Rendell.

As for the quality of the new text? It gets off to a bad start. In the first sentence of the text we learn that Poe was born in "one of the Southern states." Yes, he was: a southern state of New England: Massachusetts. (Oddly enough, the old **Murder Book** had things right.) The text then goes into a discussion of slavery in America and its effect on Poe--which I would estimate as a shade larger than zero. Elsewhere, the authors place Rochester, the **a clef** site of **Edwin Drood**, on the Thames. And I note that the caption for **A Coffin for Dimitrios** reverses matters between Sidney and Peter.

But such errors are uncommon, and I should not nitpick. I cannot judge much of the text, since I am much less interested in the sensational side than are la Cour and Mogensen, and I don't know all the minor people mentioned. But what I can judge seems accurate, though written down for the market.

Illustrations. Obviously, the concept of illustrations has changed. **The Murder Book** still looked longingly up at the reference shelf, but the new book has crawled squarely onto the middle of the coffee-table. Stress is now on film stills and frames, and on lurid jackets with any God's quantity of men slugging one another, shooting one another, staring at corpses or women--all much the same. No longer present are the nice portraits of E.C. Bentley, F.W. Crofts, Eric Ambler, and Agatha Christie. Nor will you see again that wonderful snapshot of a bleary-eyed Raymond Chandler, sitting on a bed, glared at contemptuously by Billy Wilder. Nor the fascinating group photo of Simenon and four actors who played Maigret--English, German, Italian, Dutch--at an unveiling. In its place is a dark, muddy shot of someone, somewhere, at the same ceremony.

On the whole, **The Murder Book** was superior to **Kavalkade** in illustration, but there are occasional new items that are very worth while. One is a color reproduction of a miniature of Doyle's first wife. As anyone who has studied Doyle knows, pictures of her are hard to come by, and I don't recall seeing this one before. Another is the jacket illustration, also inside, of a portrait of Dorothy Sayers that looks like She-Who-Must-Be-Obeyed after a particularly hard night. It's amusingly horrible. Another is a shot from **From Russia with Love**, showing Daniela Bianchi in bed ....

The big question. Should you buy an English-language version of this book if you still have the old? I find it hard to say yes or no. It is a borderline situation, for, as said above, the overlap between the two books is large. I probably wouldn't buy it, unless the price were very low. This would seem unlikely, what with all the color work. Someone else, though, might feel differently.

For those who don't have **The Murder Book**--newcomers to the field, libraries who missed out before, necktie-rich Christmas-presentee mystery buffs--if you don't mind the coffee-table approach and like to browse through pictures for their own sakes, you may get your money's worth. As for libraries, I think that the loss of information between editions is a flaw. All in all, I would give the new la Cour-Mogensen a limited recommendation. The authors must forgive me if I cannot wax enthusiastic. (E.F. Bleiler)

Margaret Truman. **Murder at the Smithsonian.** Arbor House, 1983, $14.95.
George Kennedy. **Murder on Location.** Avon, 1983, $2.95.

The field of crime and mystery fiction has a surprisingly long tradition of "celebrity" detective novels. Among the bylines that have appeared over the years are actor George Sanders, opera singer Helen Traubel, burlesque star Gypsy Rose Lee, early TV personality Dagmar, and (more recently) journalist and TV William F. Buckley, Jr., and comedian-composer Steve Allen. Most of these books have shared two expected characteristics: they have employed specialized backgrounds in which the author is presumed expert, and (aside from Buckley and Allen, who have track records as writers) they have been produced with the help of ghost writers.

The two Sanders novels, for example: **Crime on My Hands** (1944), a comic mystery with a Hollywood movie-making background and the ostensible author himself acting as detective, was actually written by Craig Rice and Cleve Cartmill. **Stranger at Home** (1946), more of a straight suspense novel, was in fact the work of novelist-screenwriter Leigh Brackett. Rice, a highly popular mystery writer of the forties who has fallen into critical and publishing oblivion in recent years, was also responsible for the two mysteries signed by Lee, **The G-String**

Murders (1941) and **Mother Finds a Body** (1942). Traubel's **Metropolitan Opera Murders** (1951) was ghosted by Harold Q. Masur. Paperback veteran Lou Cameron was the pen behind Dagmar's sixties spy novels.

The two examples of the celebrity mystery now under consideration can, in the absence of any evidence to the contrary, be assumed to be the work of their supposed authors, both of whom have previous writing experience.

Former First Daughter Margaret Truman, who entered the field in 1980 with **Murder in the White House**, contributes her fourth Washington-based detective novel with **Murder in the Smithsonian** As before, she combines a knowledgeable and detailed (sometimes over-detailed) view of the nation's capital with a complicated mystery plot, this time involving the bizarre murder of an art historian during a reception at the Smithsonian Institution's National Museum of Art. The site of the crime is the Foucault pendulum and the weapon is Thomas Jefferson's sword. The principal characters are Heather McBean, the victim's Scottish fiancee, and Captain Mac Hanrahan, chief of detectives of the Washington police. Others involved (all fictitious) range as high as Vice-President William Oxenhauer. This is a stronger novel than Truman's first.

Actor George Kennedy follows the lead of the two Lee novels and Sanders' **Crime on My Hands** by making himself a character in his first mystery novel, **Murder on Location**, an honorable effort though not an unqualified success. A series of murders by a variety of ingenious methods strikes a big-budget western movie on location in Mexico. In this case, some real people appear as characters, including Dean Martin, Raquel Welch, Yul Brenner, Glen Ford (who does some armchair sleuthing of his own at one point), Genevieve Bujold, and Mariette Hartley, but unsurprisingly none of these are ever under serious suspicion. There are plenty of fictitious film folk to fill the suspect roll. The background is strongly depicted, and Kennedy offers some humorous observations on both the movie business and other aspects of contemporary life. The main problem is that some of the characters (especially a pernicious TV commentator and a rock singer who speaks Valley Girl slang) are too exaggerated and one-dimensional for credibility.

Kennedy, a licensed pilot who includes some flying sequences in this book, is reportedly working on a second mystery with an aviation background. It will be worth watching for. (Jon L. Breen)

Sara Woods. **The Lie Direct**. St. Martin's, 1983, $10.95.
Erle Stanley Gardner. **The Case of the Buried Clock**. Ballantine, $2.25.

Playwrights, novelists, and TV and film scripters have long recognized the inherent drama of the courtroom, and they have provided the reading and viewing public with a long tradition of fictional trials. In the mystery field, numerous writers have made a specialty of the courtroom: Britons like Henry Cecil, Michael Underwood, Roderick Jeffries, and Edward Grierson; Americans like Arthur Train and Erle Stanley Gardner.

One of the longest running current series of legal detective stories is Sara Woods' Antony Maitland saga, of which the thirty-eighth volume is **The Lie Direct**, a title like all of the author's drawn from the works of Shakespeare. This time, barrister Maitland is briefed at the last possible moment to defend John Ryder, accused of arranging meetings between a Russian agent and an admitted (now deceased) British traitor. Dr. Boris Gollnow, ready to defect to the United

Kingdom, and a woman who claims to be Ryder's wife (making him an accused bigamist as well as a traitor) both identify him. Though everyone assumes the prosecution's case is open and shut, Maitland gradually begins to feel a gigantic frameup is in progress. Woods does courtroom scenes very effectively, and this is one of the best of her recent novels. Still, Antony gets surprising latitude from both the judge and the prosecutor in his final drive for the truth. In courtroom fiction, objections sometimes come according to their convenience to the author.

The most renowned American courtroom specialist, Gardner, has been an unfashionable mystery writer in recent years, but Ballantine continues to bring out his novels in paperback. The 1943 entry, **The Case of the Buried Clock,** has some effective courtroom give-and-take as well as one of Gardner's cleverest puzzle plots, especially attractive to devotees of the perfect alibi. Many readers may decide it's time to come back to Perry Mason, and cries of "Incompetent, irrelevant, and immaterial!" will again ring out in the land. (Jon L. Breen)

Loren D. Estleman. **The Glass Highway.** Houghton, Mifflin, 1983, $13.95.

Fictional private eyes used to be concentrated in a few American cities--Los Angeles, San Francisco, New York, and Chicago. Brett Halliday's Mike Shayne, operating out of Miami, was the odd man out. In recent years, writers in the Dashiell Hammett-Raymond Chandler tradition have gone in for more variety in urban background, and there are now series shamuses based in Boston (Robert B. Parker's Spenser), Seattle (Richard Hoyt's John Denson), Atlanta (Ralph Dennis's Hardman), Indianapolis (Michael Z. Lewin's Albert Sampson), and Cincinnati (Jonathan Valin's Harry Stoner), among other major cities.

Loren D. Estleman's Amos Walker, who now appears in his fourth book-length case, is Detroit's contribution to the ranks. Only the well-realized Motor City background is original. Walker is a traditional private eye who talks and acts tough, gets hit over the head, has both booze and roscoe in his office drawer, follows a Quixotic code or honor, gets his license pulled, and fills us in on his dreams. Estleman seems to have ignored few hard-boiled traditions. There's the corrupt suburban community (here called Iroquois Heights), comparable to Chandler's Bay City. There are patches of creative slang. (One character tells Walker, "Even the Al Kaline of hit men can wear lead from a punk with a Saturday Night Buster and the price of a lid in his pocket.") There's a great part for a young Lauren Bacall; official opponents that are vain and venal; a terrifyingly efficient hired killer; even a lady in a lake. It's a guided tour of private-eye-land.

From the first page, when Walker tells a TV station guard who asks him for two pieces of information, "I'm here to see someone, not cash a check," it's clear that Estleman has the Chandleresque prose and wisecracking dialogue down pat. The book is full of quotable descriptions. ("The desk was chromium and pressed sawdust under a plastic woodgrain veneer, without drawers or front or side panels. It had legs.") Estleman writes as well as the much-touted Robert B. Parker and offers something Parker rarely does: a well-constructed and satisfactorily complicated plot. It starts with a local anchorman (whose "hair was sprayed hard as a carp and didn't move") asking Walker to find his son. It winds up in the middle of the Detroit drug trade.

Estleman, a writer with a special talent for pastiche, has also published several westerns and two ersatz Baker Street ventures,

Sherlock Holmes vs. Dracula and **Dr. Jekyll and Mr. Holmes**. He does a good Conan Doyle, but his Chandler is even better. (Jon L. Breen)

John Dickson Carr. **The Dead Sleep Lightly.** Doubleday/Crime Club, 1983, $11.95.

Radio drama has enjoyed a mild renaissance in recent years, highlighted by the long run of the recently defunct **CBS Radio Mystery Theatre**, revivals of vintage programs on record and tape, and some new productions on Public Radio stations. Still, the publication of a book of collected radio scripts from the forties and fifties comes as a surprise. Less so, however, when the author is the late John Dickson Carr, one of the greatest writers of detective fiction's Golden Age and probably the greatest of all radio suspense scripters.

Carr was a staunch advocate of fair play, all clues on the table, from first to last. He was an unflinching admirer of such old-timers of the mystery as Jacques Futrelle, Carolyn Wells, and Thomas W. Hanshew, authors who shared his love of the seemingly impossible (but logically explained) occurrence. An American fascinated with things British, Carr so loved his adopted English home that he returned there even after the outbreak of World War II, staying on to write BBC plays and propaganda messages despite repeated brushes with death and destruction. (Only the election of a Labour government was enough to make him leave, and the re-election of the Conservatives drew him back.) A writer of great versatility, he made a mark as a true-crime writer (**The Murder of Sir Edmund Godfrey**), a biographer (**The Life of Sir Arthur Conan Doyle**), a reviewer ("The Jury Box" column in **Ellery Queen's Mystery Magazine**), a short-story writer, and a novelist.

Carr was a prolific writer, producing novels at a four-a-year pace in the thirties under his own name and the thinly-disguised pseudonym, Carter Dickson. In his later years, he employed his series detectives less frequently and pioneered the historical detective novel, setting his tales in the past times that had always fascinated him. His last novel was **The Hungry Goblin** (1972), a Victorian tale in which **Moonstone**-author Wilkie Collins acts as detective. From that time until his death in 1977, Carr confined his activities to reviewing.

In 1980, Douglas G. Greene, a professor of history at Old Dominion University, edited **The Door to Doom** (Harper and Row), a gathering of shorter Carr works, most of them previously uncollected in book form. The centerpiece of this volume was a group of stories from the twenties, featuring the French police sleuth Bencolin, central figure of Carr's earliest novels. Originally published in a college journal, the **Haverfordian**, these stories were unknown even to most detective fiction specialists. Green also included essays, pulp horror stories from the thirties, Sherlockian parodies, a Carr bibliography, and six fine radio mysteries.

In the present collection, Greene adds nine more radio dramas, all of them in their British versions (though some appeared on radio in America as well) and two starring the great detective Carr based on G.K. Chesterton, Dr. Gideon Fell. Reading these scripts, effective enough on the printed page, one can imagine how beautifully they must have played on the radio, preferably heard in front of the fireplace with a storm brewing outside. Consider the tantalizing situations. In "The Black Minute," a medium is stabbed to death in mid-seance, though the room is locked from the inside and all the other inhabitants (fortunately including Dr. Fell) are joined hand-to-hand. In "The Devil's Saint," a prospective suitor accepts his potential father-in-law's challenge to spend the night in a room that has proven fatal to all previous occupants. In "The Dead Sleep Lightly," a publisher seemingly makes a phone call to a dead woman--on a disconnected phone. In "The Devil's Manuscript," freely adapted from an Ambrose Bierce story, an author of ghost stories claims he has written a tale so terrifying as to frighten its reader to death. The other five scripts offer similar problems, all satisfactorily and ingeniously worked out while being as generous in clues as they are in atmosphere.

Greene's fine eleven-page introduction not only prepares the reader for the wonders of the nine scripts but gives some impression of what a remarkable man Carr must have been, a natural subject for full-scale biographical treatment in some future volume.

Jane Dentinger. **Murder on Cue.** Doubleday/Crime Club, 1983, $11.95.

In 1971, two distinguished scholars and mystery buffs, Jacques Barzun and Wendell Hertig Taylor, produced an entertaining, infuriating, unreliable, and indispensable critical bibliography of mystery fiction called **A Catalogue of Crime.** The pair admit to a bias in favor of the old-fashioned formal detective puzzle, and they have strong ideas about what elements make for a good mystery novel. They have an aversion to theatrical whodunits. In discussing Ngaio Marsh's **Night at the Vulcan,** they state, "The stage often brings out the worst in Ngaio"--many of her readers would claim the exact opposite is the case. About Lenore Glen Offord's **Walking Shadow:** "There's the usual hanky-panky about a theater ...." Holly Roth's **Crimson in the Purple** is "not in the top class" as "is often true when actors and playwrights and 'dramatic' atmosphere are mixed with murder on or off stage." Though they praise a fair number of theatrical mysteries, the good results are usually credited despite the background, not because of it.

I couldn't disagree more with Barzun and Taylor in their attitude to theatrical mysteries. For me, a theater is an irresistible, sure-fire locale for fictional murder. (Others are hospitals, schools and colleges, trains, ships, planes, and other conveyances.) And lately actors have been some of the more promising new fictional sleuths. One of the best series to debut in recent years stars Simon Brett's Charles Paris, whose cases are less notable for their plots than for the satirical insider's view of British show business. Another British acting detective to star in a series of books is Anne Morice's Tessa Crichton, married to a policeman but usually inclined to investigate on her own.

American writers have introduced their own actor-detectives: Linda J. Barnes' Michael Spraggue debuted in **Blood Will Have Blood** (Avon, 1982), while David Snell's Osgood Bass had his first (and so far only) case in **Lights, Camera ... Murder** (St. Martin's, 1979). But not until Jane Dentinger's Jocelyn O'Roarke have we had an American theatrical detective to rival Paris.

The professionally-struggling Jocelyn gets a job as understudy to aging leading lady Harriet Weldon in a courtroom drama called **Term of Trial.** It soon develops, gratifyingly if embarrassingly, that Jocelyn is much better in the part than the first-stringer, who is subsequently found dead in her dressing room. Is it murder? The characters in the book may wonder, but they lack the reader's advantages, such as knowing the title. There is no shortage of possible killers in a case that is resolved most fairly and satisfactorily in an old-fashioned gathering of the suspects.

Dentinger's first mystery has the same combination of wit, incisive characterization, and knowledgeable theatrical background found in Brett's series. If she is not yet quite as scintillating a stylist as Brett, she may be a somewhat more skilled plotter. Herself an actress with off-Broadway and regional theater experience, Dentinger knows her setting well and can convey effectively the joys and tensions of preparing a play for production. (Jon L. Breen)

Simon Brett. **Murder in the Title.** Scribner's, 1983. 191 pp.

A character in this book explains the choice of a rather fourth-rate play by saying that any play with murder in the title will bring a big audience. Perhaps that is so. It is definitely so that anything written by Simon Brett will bring an enjoyable reading session. Here, as always, Brett's characters are superbly drawn, especially his series characters, of which Charles Paris is the star. Brett's theater settings are varied and lively. Usually, the plot is clever, although often less effective than the characterization and the setting. The plot is in fact weak in **Murder in the Title.**

The image of poor old Charles having the role of a dead (as in deceased) person in a bad play in a small town has irony that is not the least subtle. That deceased character with the drunken giggles is perfect. Charles "does a corpse" as a corpse. Also perfect and typical is the fact that, although Charles has landed the worst possible role in which to demonstrate any talent, he alone of the cast and their attachments is perceptive about why this silly play is getting a run and what evil lurks between the lines and behind the scenes.

The problem with the plot is that it is apparent very early just who is the culprit and even why. This is stated by a reader whose rate of figuring out whodunits before the final page is about 2.6 percent!

Still, it's Brett, and it's fun. (Martha Alderson)

James Crumley. **Dancing Bear.** Random House, 1983, 228 pp., $12.95.

The earliest American private-eye characters were portrayed as tough-guy professionals, the antithesis to the gentlemen amateur detectives of the Sherlock Holmes tradition. But, thanks to the Lew Archer novels of the late Ross Macdonald, the contemporary PI tends to be more in Alan Alda's image than in Bogart's: a man sensitive to feelings, full of inner torment, slow to use force. It's this newer tradition that has been both explored and extended to its limits by James Crumley, whose two earlier crime novels--**The Wrong Case** (1975) and **The Last Good Kiss** (1978)--were quite simply the finest private-eye books of the decade, and whose third and latest is only slightly less good.

Crumley's setting is the bleak magnificence of western Montana and his prevailing mood a wacked-out post-Vietnam empathy with all sorts of dopers, dropouts, losers and loonies, the human wreckage of the institutionalized butchery we call the real world. His protagonist Milodragovitch, last seen in **The Wrong Case,** is a cocaine addict and a boozer, the child of two suicides, a compulsive womanizer like his wealthy, Hemingwayesque father, a man literally marking time until his fifty-second birthday, when he'll inherit the family fortune which his pioneer ancestors legally stole from the Indians. He is also the purest Jesus figure in the history of detective fiction, and the most reverent toward the earth and its creatures. Such a person is unlikely to be a roaring success as a private investigator, and Crumley knows he can't be and doesn't pretend that he is. In **Dancing Bear** an old girlfriend of his father's draws Milo into combat against a multinational corporation dumping toxic waste into the ground water. Along the way there's a great deal of graphic violence and sweetly casual sex and endless drives through mountain snowscapes as Milo and his buddy, the crazed Viet vet Simmons, snort coke and guzzle alcohol and thrash around trying to find out what kind of bloody mess they've gotten themselves into. They never learn the whole story nor do we, for Crumley's interest in plot is faint and his sense of structure all but non existent.

But his powers with character and language and relationship and incident are so uncanny that he can afford to jettison plot mechanics and explanations. What makes his books live in the reader's mind and blood is the accumulation of dozens of small crazy encounters, full of "confusion and muddle, disorder and despair." He can have Milo visit a graceful mansion to interview a wealthy old client in a plant-filled solarium, and make us forget we ever read the famous greenhouse scene in Raymond Chandler's novel **The Big Sleep**. He can punctuate the detective's quest with short bursts of the staples of PI fiction, sex and gore, and make each one fresh and vivid and unforgettable. He can move us to accept the dregs of the human race as our brothers, to feel the rape of the earth. As Chandler said of Dashiell Hammett, he can write scenes that seem never to have been written before.

If **Dancing Bear** seems not quite up to Crumley's two earlier crime novels, it's only because huge chunks of it, superbly set on paper though they are, have nothing to do with what's going on in the book. Aimlessly meandering storyline and all, it's still one of the finest PI exploits of the past fifteen years. Those who haven't yet discovered Crumley should start with **The Wrong Case** and **The Last Good Kill** and save this new one for later. Those who do know him will need no encouragement from a reviewer to grab **Dancing Bear** at once. (Francis M. Nevins, Jr.)

Roderic Jeffries. **Deadly Petard.** St. Martin's, 1983, $10.95.

Inspector Enrique Alvarez of the Mallorcan police is an interesting, rather slothful character who has won praise from the critics in his previous four cases. He seems to be in continual conflict with the English tourists and inhabitants of the island, yet he is not about to let them upset his routing of drink, food, and sleep. Much like Leo Bruce's Sergeant Beef, his manner and exterior is misleading. By the end of the book we know that Alvarez rather than his antagonistic superior or the brash, eager British detective is the only one sharp enough to untangle the puzzle.

Presented in an almost inverted form, the plot is simple enough on the face of it. Gertrude Dean, a semi-successful artist, has committed suicide out of a fear of cancer. Too coincidentally, one of her oldest and closest friends lost his wife a few years before in exactly the same circumstances. And he was not only the chief beneficiary under Gertrude's will, he also did not want her to let out a secret from his past.

There is little detection as such, and the story more or less unfolds rather than develops. A bit of misdirection and a traditional British attitude and style distract from the major clues. Author Jeffries (pseudonym of Jeffrey Ashford) provides a polished, relaxing story with an ironic ending that finally explains the title. (Fred Dueren)

The Documents In the Case (Letters)

From Louise Gagnon, 1425-1577 Lawrence Ave. W., Toronto, Ontario, CANADA M6L 1C4:

I find rather amusing those correspondents who "never" read a particular type of book, thereby probably cutting themselves off from a lot of enjoyment. I have eclectic tastes, reading English "cozies" (a recent favourite being Martha Grimes), police procedurals, PI novels (though, unlike Bob Randisi, Spenser would be at the top of my list), humourous fiction such as Michael Kenyon's books featuring Inspector Peckover, etc. Even those types such as espionage or thrillers which I am generally not that fond of feature some authors whose work I never miss. My favourite writer of any type is Anthony Price, whose way with words is always a joy to read.

At the moment I am reading a lot of novels based on true crimes. A book which I highly recommend is **The Man Who Died Twice**, by Samuel Peeples. It is a fictional recreation of the murder of William Desmond Taylor and, the evocation of early Hollywood is beautifully done.

From Howard W. Sharpe, P.O. Box 204, St. Kilda, Victoria, AUSTRALIA 3182:

Last year I came across a Ballantine paperback, **The Carlos Contract**, by David Atlee Phillips, published in 1980. Since the name so closely resembles Philip Atlee's name (James Atlee Phillips), I assume there is some relation between them. Can you or anyone else tell me anything about this? The book is very good indeed. I don't know if David Atlee Phillips has written other books, but I hope that either he has or will do.

From William F. Deeck, 9020 Autoville Drive, College Park, MD 20740:

In Barry Van Tilburg's "Spy Series Characters in Hardback, Part XIV," Mr. Van Tilburg, in dealing with Charlie Muffin, says under "Other Comments" that Charlie's wife was killed in the first book in mistake for him and that is what threw him on the run. The version I have of **Charlie M** in paperback has Mrs. Muffin hale and hearty at the end of the book. Also, Charlie was on the run because he had absconded with $500,000 belonging to the CIA.

Incidentally, PBS had a video presentation of **Charlie Muffin** on the other evening. It was not a bad adaptation, in my opinion, but that may be because it has been a while since I have read the book. Anyhow, the casting was excellent, which seems to be a hallmark of British films.

I'm not sure when Marvin Lachman wrote his review of **Nevsky's Return**. Obviously he missed the news a couple of months ago about **Nevsky's Demon** allegedly being a plagiarism of a novel by John D. MacDonald. The last report I heard was that Gat had apologized to MacDonald and **Nevsky's Demon** had been pulled back from the bookstores. I didn't keep the articles on this, so my information is basic. Maybe Mr. Lachman would like to follow up on this, and maybe **Nevsky's Demon** will become a collector's item for those fortunate few who had a chance to buy it.

A list of favorite private eyes? I'm not sure I can come up with ten, but I'll give it a try because there's one who will never make anyone else's list and I think he should get at least one vote. Here goes:

Ross H. Spencer's Chance Purdue
Michael Lewin's Albert Samson
Dashiell Hammett's Continental Op
Jonathan Valin's Harry Stoner
P.B. Yuill's James Hazell
Frank Norman's Ed Nelson

Sorry, but that's it. Two Britishers and the one who will get no other votes--good old Chance. Anyhow, the limited list will give you some idea that I am not generally enamored of private eyes. I'll stick with the amateurs and the police.

P.S. I wasn't going to append a list of favorite novels since I dread ridicule. But I reconsidered, even though I think such lists are idiosyncratic and, in my case certainly, eclectic. A much better list would be favorite authors or favorite characters, thus giving writers who may not have written a classic but who have a body of superior novels a chance.

1. **Warrant for X**, by Philip MacDonald
2. **Ten Little Indians**, by Agatha Christie (or whichever title you may prefer of the three)
3. **Ten Days' Wonder**, by Ellery Queen
4. **The Burning Court**, by John Dickson Carr
5. **Night at the Mocking Widow**, by Carter Dickson
6. **The Caves of Steel**, by Isaac Asimov
7. **Love Lies Bleeding**, by Edmund Crispin
8. **What a Body!**, by Alan Green
9. **When the Wind Blows**, by Cyril Hare
10. **The Last Known Address**, by Joseph Harrington
11. **The Last Doorbell**, by Joseph Harrington
12. **The Saint Maker**, by Leonard Holton
13. **Yellowthread Street**, by William Marshall
14. **A Death at the Bar**, by Charles Drummond
15. **Dover One**, by Joyce Porter

From Fred Isaac, 1501 Milvia St., Berkeley, CA 94709:

I'm at the end of the reading sessions for a variety of projects. One is a profile of Marcia Muller, whose **Tree of Death** is due out in the next couple of weeks. (I expect I have become the Bay Area person; the piece I did on Bill Pronzini is due in **Clues**.) And I am also about to see Collin Wilcox for a chapter in Earl and George's forthcoming **Cops and Constables** another companion to the **Women (etc.) of Mystery**.

There were some items in the back issues that I want to comment on, before they sink too far into the past. First, Bob Randisi's list of PI's ought to be followed by a series of warnings. I have no objection to the names he put on it, or the ones (Parker in particular) he leaves off. But saying that these are THE BEST suggests that the newcomer can do away with everyone else. I have the feeling that the compilers of the two major collections (Scene of the Crime and Murder Ink) are doing all of us a disservice by their selections. It's one thing for Bob to tell us what he thinks, and another for us to take his word unquestioningly. Allan Hubin, in **The Mystery Story** (edited by John Ball) lists scores of operatives, and some of them are real gems. Since we found our way into this field by reading, we could do worse than try some forgotten series, and reviving it for others.

[While we all like to flatter ourselves on our excellent taste, the truth is that every person's list of "Bests" is actually only a list of "Favorites"—the favorites of the person making the list. I happen to believe that Strong Poison and Red Harvest are both excellent books, but I dare say that many—if not most—of the people who read and like one of these books either will not read or, if they do read, will not like the other. The problem comes from confusing in our own minds what is excellent and what we like. I cheerfully admit to liking a great deal that is not excellent, and I would put one or two (or maybe more) less-than-excellent books on my list of favorite novels. As for those pompous asses who feel superior enough to enumerate the ten worst novels of all time and then select those ten from the productions of Margery Allingham, E.C. Bentley, John Dickson Carr, Raymond Chandler, Agatha Christie, Arthur Conan Doyle, Robert Littell, Ngaio Marsh, Dorothy L. Sayers, and Rex Stout—if the shoe fits, Dilys, wear it—the less said, the better.]

Much more frustrating is the letter/article from Melinda Reynolds on women writers (7:2) and Teri White's agreement (7:3). My gripe with them both is that they seem to have read narrowly. I liken their put-down to Edmund Wilson's of forty years ago: "The book I started was no god, so I stopped reading." A pity. And more, too, but I'll let it go.

Enough for now, except to ask if you are interested in a piece I'm thinking of on Buckley's Blackford Oakes novels. I may get a pre-pub. of the fifth (due in January), and I may have something for you soon-ish after that. [**Sure, I'm interested—what's this I hear about Buckley having a ghost for these novels?**]

From Melinda Reynolds, Rt. 2, Box 93B, Corydon, KY 42406:

Blast it! Just received TMF July-Aug. '83, which is great, but I seem to have missed the May-June issue. I guess the PO has sent it to parts unknown (with any luck, perhaps you'll get a subscription from the person who ends up with it). I feel like I've missed a key episode in a soap opera--what's this about price increases? From $12 to $15 per year? Well, sure, why not; it's money well spent--I get a lot more than $15 worth of enjoyment from TMF. I also note opinions pro & con on paying submissions. I would think that would be an editorial decision, and if some of the contributors prefer not to be paid, then that's between you and them. You seem a capable fellow, do what you think best.

A Kaypro, huh? I looked at those, too; a neat little machine. However, I obtained an Osbourne I Double Density a while back, for $1250; a Zenith monitor ($100); and a daisy-wheel printer ($599). (And if I didn't have the thing set up doing something else at the moment, it would be typing this letter--sorry about the mess.) That was the best price I could get on a word-processing computer/printer--and now, just my luck, Osbourne has gone into bankruptcy. Ah, well--I have no complaints with the computer. It does an excellent job. It took me two days to figure it out, but we're getting along fine now. It also has something called The Source, that came with it; some type of telephone hook-up. I figure it's going to cost more money, and our phone bill is outrageous enough without yakking on the computer.

[**I had two objections to the Osbourne—the tiny screen, and the fact that it only came with WordStar, which won't support proportional-spaced printing. The price you got was a good one, but the reason it was good was that Osbourne was going under for the third time. But so long as it works for you, you are ahead of the game. As for The Source, what you probably got was an hour of free time on the network, but to use it you will have to buy a modem (at $100 or more), then if you want to continue to utilize The Source you will have to subscribe and pay an hourly rate for subsequent uses that will devastate your budget unless your last name is Getty. Its a fantastic service if you need it, but most of the info available on it isn't useful for Everyman, and the cost is generally outrageous.**]

Michael L. Cook: Uh, Guy, I think your question/observation at the end of Michael Cook's letter was a bit out of line. I don't think he's questioning John Nieminski's results, but the method used to achieve them. [**That's what makes horse races.**]

Joe R. Christopher: Sorry you took my comments of Dorothy L. Sayers to heart; my friend thought I was too hard on here, too, as, she said, I had to understand the mood and spirit of the times to fully understand Lord Peter's world and the people in it.

I came very close to reading P.D. James's **Innocent Blood** but passed it over after reading her other books; and my friend (mentioned above) also suggested I read Allingham's **Tiger in the Smoke**--so I'll check them out, along with Teri White's **Triangle**, which several other readers in TMF's letters section seemed to enjoy.

Richard S. Callagan, Jr.: I'm always reluctant to list books due to the fact that I'm not an omnivorous reader of mystery fiction (or of any other kind, for that matter; I read what I like, discard what I don't). My mystery reading is restricted to a very select group of authors, as I have very strong likes and dislikes, and if I read one type of mystery or detective fiction, I usually stay with the same authors.

But, since you asked, here's a list of my favorites, from the books I have read:

1. Dick Francis--This gentleman is incapable of writing an inferior book.
2. A. Conan Doyle--What can I say about Sherlock Holmes? Reading the Holmes Canon for the first time is like your first love.
3. Ellery Queen--The most notable thing to me about the Queen books (aside from the convoluted plots) is Ellery's evolution from a smugly prissy dilettante of crime to a more mature, insightful, and sensitive individual. And, anyway, I adore Inspector Queen.
4. Rex Stout--Stands head and shoulders, knees, even, above other detective "teams" due entirely to Wolfe's indomitable & insufferable character and the relationship between him and the wonderfully marvelous Archie Goodwin.

5. Lawrence Block--I'm not sure where Bernie Rhodenbarr would fall in the detective category, as he's more crook than detective, but the Burglar Series is refreshingly different entertainment, with just the right amount of humor.
6. Reference Books--I love reference books, especially when interviews are included. And mystery reference books seem to be the most interesting.

And, while I'm at it, I absolutely loathe:

1. Hard-boiled detective novels (what kind of language do they speak, anyway?)
2. International terrorism
3. Locked-room murders
4. Adopted children searching for parent(s)
5. Oriental detectives in any shape, manner, or form
6. Police stories.

    Fred Issac: Did the audience go along with the views expressed by the panel on the session on library material regarding mysteries? If they were mystery fans as well, seems most would be familiar with TMF & TAD, and would recognize the merits of both journals in the mystery field, especially as excellent sources of valuable information not available in the commercial magazines. [In a portion of Fred's letter (above) that I did not quote, he says: "The response was not tremendous, although Jane Bakerman made some useful points.")]
    By all means, send in the talk given at the Popular Culture meeting in Kansas; I'd like to read it.
    Jiro Kimura: Although I didn't know Jud Sapp, your comment ("He bought a copy of my picture book and thanked me for publishing it before I thanked him for buying it") says a lot.
    James R. Cullen: You're right, of course: Philo Vance **is** just as big a "silly ass" as Lord Peter, more so, I think; but the article was about women writers. I've read more disagreeable male authors than women authors, but then, I've read more books written by men; however, when it comes down to really atrocious writing (in any genre, with the possible exception of Gothic novels and Cortland Romances), male writers are hard to beat.
    What do you consider a mystery fan? I'm aware that "fan" is short for "fanatic," and I'll readily agree that I'm not fanatic about mystery novels. I simply like reading a **good** book, and a lot of mystery novels are good books; in fact, **very** good books. I watch more mysteries on TV (except **Magnum PI; T.J. Hooker,** and **Simon & Simon**--give me a break) and prefer a movie mystery to any other kind, and out of any ten books I read, five or six will be mystery or detective. I do have a narrow range of reading within the mystery field, and I don't care to waste time on something that wouldn't interest me. Everyone has favorites and preferences, that's why there's so many diverse authors on the bookstands. I'm not saying women writers are inferior--just that I haven't come across any that appeal to me. I'll take your advice and try Patricia Highsmith and June Thomson later on, after I finish Teri White's **Triangle.**
    Linda Toole: You're welcome; and thanks for your kind comments. Perhaps later, after another reading bout, I'll submit "Women Mystery Writers Revisited." I'll also add Lucille Kallen to my "to be read eventually" list.
    Back to you, Guy. I was wondering, if you have any space left after this monstrously long letter, if you'd consider printing the

following Dick Francis Checklist in the Letters Section. If not in the next issue, perhaps in the Nov.-Dec. issue. I've been trying to locate everything written by Francis, and where it first appeared. If it is incomplete, or in error, or if anyone has any additions (I know my info on his English articles and publications is next to nil), I would appreciate knowing about it.

NOVELS:
 Dead Cert, 1962
 Nerve, 1964
 For Kicks, 1965
 Odds Against, 1965 (U.S.: 1966)
 Flying Finish, 1966 (1967)
 Blood Sport, 1967 (1968)
 Forfeit, 1969
 Enquiry, 1969
 Rat Race, 1970 (1971)
 Bonecrack, 1971 (1972)
 Smokescreen, 1972
 Slay-ride, 1973 (1974)
 Knockdown, 1974 (1975)
 High Stakes, 1975 (1976)
 In the Frame, 1976 (1977)
 Risk   1977 (1978)
 Trial Run 1978 (1979)
 Whip Hand 1979 (1980)
 Reflex   1980 (1981)
 Twice Shy 1981 (1982)
 Banker   1982 (1983)
 The Danger 1983 (1984)
(NOTE: The Radnor-Halley Agency, formed in **Odds Against**, was mentioned in **Blood Sport** and **Knockdown**--and explained away in **Whip Hand**.)

SHORT STORIES: 1970 "Carrot for a Chestnut" (**Stories of Crime & Detection**, 1974; **Masters of Mystery—The 70's**, 1979; **Ellery Queen's Faces of Mystery**, ?)
 1973 "A Day of Wine & Roses" (**Sports Illustrated**, May 1973; as "The Big Story" in **E.Q. Crime Wave**, 1976 as "The Gift" in **Winter's Crimes 5**, 1973)
 1976 "Rip-off at Kingdom Hill" (**Classic Magazine**, June/July, 1976 [also interview in editorial column])
 1977 "Nightmare" (**E.Q. Searches & Seizures**, 1977 [Since I haven't been able to find a copy of this to read, this story may be a re-titled version of one of the other short stories.]
 1978 "21 Good Men & True" (**Verdict of 13**, 1978)
 1979 "Day of the Losers" (**Classic Magazine**, Oct./Nov., 1979; **EQMM**, 198?; **John Creasey's Crime Collection**, 1980)

CO-EDITOR:
Best Racing & Chasing Stories I, 1957
Best Racing & Chasing Stories II, 1968
Racing Man's Bedside Book, 1969

ARTICLES:
"Reality Behind the Dream," **Classic Magazine**, Feb./Mar. 1977

SCREENPLAY:
Dead Cert, 1964

TELEVISION:
"The Racing Game," based on **Odds Against:** "Odds Against"
"The Racing Game," story lines and technical advice:
   "Trackdown"
   "Gambling Lady"
   "Needle"
   "Horses for Courses"
   "Horsenap"

AUTOBIOGRAPHY:
The Sport of Queens, 1957 (revised in 1968, 1974, and 1982)

From Charles Shibuk, 2084 Bronx Park East, Bronx, NY 10462:

   I had occasion to read Rex Stout's non-criminous **Mr. Cinderella** (1938) recently, and Nero Wolfe fanciers (and trivia buffs) might be interested to learn that Sergeant Stebbins makes a brief appearance toward the end of the novel.

From True Rice, 2049 Walnut Blvd., Walnut Creek, CA 94596:

   I'm just catching up to TMF 7:2. Bob Randisi writes great books, but we do disagree when it comes to the top ten PI's. He seems to lean to the "moderns." I'm old fashioned, I guess. Herewith my own list:

   Dashiell Hammett's Continental Op
   Raymond Chandler's Philip Marlowe
   Raoul Whitfield's (Ramon Decolta) Jo Gar
   Ross Macdonald's Lew Archer
   Thomas Dewey's Mac
   Lester Dent's Oscar Sail
   Bill Pronzini's "Nameless"
   Norbert Davis's Max Latin
   Joe Gores' DKA group
   Bunches of current writers (including Bob)

   Melinda Reynolds expressed thoughts about female writers that, as a typical male chauvanist pig, I was reluctant to write about. I have long thought that Agatha Christie (with the possible exception of the Parker Pyne stories) was the dullest writer I have ever tried. Like Melinda, I can't help thinking there must be something wrong with me, since I can't see what hundreds of thousands of other readers have seen. I **do** find the work of June Thomson entertaining. (If it turns out that "Melinda Reynolds" is a pseudonym for Wallingford K. Humbert, my face will be red.)
   She also refers to the "inevitable descriptive paragraphs added to fill out the novel." I have the feeling that those paragraphs have become more and more common--or is that a complaint of a reader who can, and does, easily skip right over them?
   Your notes in 7:3 about the trials and tribulations of a computer seeker were extremely helpful. Separating facts from puffery is difficult in this field. You contributed.

patterns of life.

Like most of Yorke's central characters, Alan and Louise are victims both of circumstance and of others' coldness (Louise's mother is something less than warmly affectionate), and the two find both mutual and individual strength, despite their seeming weakness and manipulability. Savingly, Daphne Parker and Mrs. Hampton, Louise's mother, are not monsters; they are woman who have made their own lives and who expect others to summon up the strength and tenacity to do the same. In this way, Yorke just barely avoids stereotyping, just barely avoids demanding totally traditional behavior from her female characters. What she does demand from all human beings is the willingness both to talk and to listen; the fact that almost all people fail, to some degree, at both efforts is the point of compelling interest for readers and the source of energy of this and many other Yorke novels. **Devil's Work** won't surprise anyone, but it will hold readers' interest; it's a neat, workerlike job. (Jane S. Bakerman)

Sue Grafton. **"A" Is for Alibi**. Holt, Rinehart and Winston, 1982, 208 pp.

The dust jacket of **"A" Is for Alibi** introduces Sue Grafton as the author of **Keziah Dane** and **The Lolly Madonna War**, as a screenwriter, and as the creator of "a new mystery series featuring Kinsey Millhone, an ex-cop who likes her work and works alone." Grafton is a good writer and Millhone is a good character; I hope the series works kits way right through the alphabet and back.

Grafton's plot is taut, fast-moving, and absorbing: newly released from prison, Nikki Fife, who was convicted for murdering her husband, hires Kinsey Millhone to find out who really done it. Realistically pessimistic about the viability of eight-year-old clues and witnesses whose memories are probably clouded not only by self-interest but also by the passage of time, Millhone undertakes the case and sets out to find the killer. Along the way, she meets fascinating characters and confirms what she already suspects: few people are really what they seem to be; offering trust and affection is a dangerous, though necessary, part of human business; and that shoe doesn't like killing--"Killing feels odd to me," she says, in brilliant and therefore convincing understatement. In a brief, compelling preface, Millhone states outright that the official police statement about the shooting and the report for her own files which she has already written up have not eased her spirit, have not helped her set her world back into operating order--"The language in both documents is neutral, the terminology oblique, and neither says quite enough." In the body of her narrative, she sets that right: the language is direct; the feeling is personal but never whining or sentimental; and the impact is "quite enough."

LIKE a host of tough, disenchanted private eyes before her, Kinsey operates in Southern California--Santa Teresa; and like Spade and Archer and all their other descendants, she is a loner--"You try to keep life simple but it never works, and in the end all you have left is yourself."

Personally strong but aware of her own shortcomings, physically tough and able to absorb punishment on mean streets and beaches, Millhone is also literate, candid, and introspective. She's very well worth meeting. (Jane S. Bakerman)

www.ingramcontent.com/pod-product-compliance
Lightning Source LLC
Chambersburg PA
CBHW031309060426
42444CB00032B/820